W9-BSJ-542

LIPS TOGETHER, TEETH APART

BY TERRENCE McNALLY

★

★

DRAMATISTS
PLAY SERVICE
INC.

LIPS TOGETHER, TEETH APART
Copyright © 1992, Terrence McNally

All Rights Reserved

SPECIAL NOTE

SPECIAL NOTE ON SONGS AND RECORDINGS

For Wendy Wasserstein

LIPS TOGETHER, TEETH APART was first presented at the Manhattan Theatre Club (Lynne Meadow, Artistic Director; Barry Grove, Managing Director) in New York City on May 28, 1991. It was directed by John Tillinger; the set design was by John Lee Beatty; the costume design was by Jane Greenwood; the lighting design was by Ken Billington; the sound design was by Stewart Werner; the fight staging was by Jerry Mitchell and the production stage manager was Pamela Singer. The cast was as follows:

CHLOE HADDOCK ....Christine Baranski
SAM TRUMAN ....Nathan Lane
JOHN HADDOCK .... Anthony Heald
SALLY TRUMAN .... Swoosie Kurtz

THE PLAYERS

SAM TRUMAN, a self-employed businessman

SALLY TRUMAN, his wife

JOHN HADDOCK, head of admissions at a boy's prep school

CHLOE HADDOCK, his wife, Sam's older sister

THE SETTING

The wooden deck of a summer beach house on Long Island.

At the rear of the stage and well behind our principal playing area, sliding glass/screen doors in the center of the house open onto the cooking/dining area. People inside the house can be seen as they prepare a meal, eat, make a phone call, etc., even though the parts of the play we can actually hear and participate in all take place on the wooden deck outside the house itself. The same goes for the bedrooms. There are bedrooms to each side of this central kitchen/dining wing which can be reached from either inside the house or through sliding glass/screen doors that open onto the deck. As with the cooking/dining area, people may also be seen, if not heard, when they are in their bedrooms, unless their blinds are specifically drawn. The master bedroom is stage right. Another, smaller bedroom is stage left. There is a locked door next to the stage left bedroom. We cannot see into the room behind it.

The deck itself is furnished with chairs, a picnic table and benches, chaises for sunning, and a charcoal grill. There is also a swimming pool, though perhaps we see only a corner of it. The pool is lit for the last scene. There is an outdoor shower with a half-door for privacy. Finally, there are steps leading down from the deck to the dunes on which the house is built. Throughout the play, except in the last scene, there is a steady sea breeze. Things will blow in it. A

Japanese silk fish will be inflated by it. Paper napkins will blow away. The roar of the ocean is steady. Sooner or later, we will get used to it.

THE TIME

The time of the play is now. It is Fourth of July weekend.

LIPS TOGETHER, TEETH APART

ACT ONE

AT RISE: Tableau—Sally painting at easel, Chloe standing at the kitchen sink, within, John reading a newspaper, Sam testing the chlorine level in the pool.

No one moves. Silence.

Music begins. The farewell trio from Mozart's Così fan tutte. As the trio progresses, the stage and the actors will slowly come to "life."

The first movement will be the gentle stirrings of an ornamental flag in the early morning breeze.

Then Sally will begin to paint, Chloe to drink coffee in the kitchen, John to turn the pages of his New York Times, Sam to retrieve the chlorine indicator—but all in time to the music, not reaching naturalistic behavior until the end of the piece.

By the time the trio ends, we will be in "real" time.

CHLOE. Is anyone still hungry? Does anyone want more? I've got eggs, bacon, bagels, Sara Lee, Entenmann's, fresh-squeezed orange juice, coffee, decaf (Colombian water processed), Special K, English muffins, French muffins, Dutch muffins, German muffins. Hello?

SAM. It looks clean. It looks immaculate. I can see right to the bottom. Somebody's been around. His friend must have kept up the pool service. I'm very impressed.

JOHN. It says here eleven percent of this country is black. That's amazing. I would have thought it was more like fifty.

SALLY. I can see why people do still lifes. The light keeps changing.

Every time I look up it's different. I'd be better off making the whole thing up. I think that's what the really great artists did anyway. I mean, whoever saw wheat fields like yellow ropes until van Gogh did? Well not "ropes" maybe; big fat squiggles of yellow paint he just squirted out of the tube.

CHLOE. Sometimes I wonder who we're really talking to.

JOHN. Whom we're really talking to, Petal.

CHLOE. They all heard me say "Is anyone still hungry? Does anyone want more?" Then why don't they answer? Apathy? Actual dislike? It was a simple question. I mean, I didn't ask "Does anybody know what the meaning of life is?" or "Are you sleeping with my husband, Sally?" or "Does anybody remember how late that little grocery store down by the ferry stays open?" All I asked was "Is anyone still hungry? Does anyone want more?" There's times like this, if I had a small hand gun I'd use it. Tiny little pops. Pop! pop! pop! All fall down.

> *Sally has stopped painting. She is watching someone on the beach in front of the house. None of the other three pays her any attention.*

JOHN. Doesn't this country seem more than eleven percent black to you?

SAM. Not where you live. I'd say it seems more like zero percent, which is probably why you live there. *(To Sally.)* Where do you think they might have kept the chlorine, Sal, in case we need any?

SALLY. I don't know.

JOHN. Try the utility shed.

SAM. What's a utility shed?

JOHN. A shed for utilities.

SAM. I'm sorry. You're talking to a humble Trenton, New Jersey, homeowner here. I keep everything in the garage. So where would I find this famous utility shed?

JOHN. They're usually under the house.

SAM. I bet I know where that is: under the house! Okay, okay, so I'm not Henny Youngman but you all thought I was pretty funny last night when I fell off that boardwalk hauling all those groceries in that little red wagon. What do these people have against cars and sidewalks?

CHLOE. It's an island.

SAM. So's Manhattan. They drive and walk all over the place.

CHLOE. And look at Manhattan. I don't care what anyone says. This is paradise. They want to keep it that way. Sally, it's heaven. The house, the setting. I am green.

She comes over to Sally and squints at her painting.

What is it or should I be able to tell?

SALLY. That. *(Nods towards the ocean.)*

CHLOE. That is that? Oh, I see. Very clever. What do you call that? Abstract Expressionism? Pop Cubism? What?

SALLY. It's nothing, right now. I'll tell you when it's finished.

CHLOE. *(To Sam and John.)* Sshh, genius at work. Have we seen our neighbors yet?

SAM. You mean the boys from Ipanema next door? No. They're still getting their beauty sleep.

CHLOE. I'm sure they'll be very nice. I did a little research: It's strictly *crème de la crème* here. We should all have a wonderful brother like David to leave us something like this.

Sam pulls something on a string out of the pool.

SAM. According to this gauge, the water is perfect. The question is: Do we trust a gauge? I'm sorry but I'm very sensitive about pools. Our mother was very big on polio. And this was after they'd come up with a cure for it. She was ready for it to make a big comeback. Grow up like that and you view a pool or a public toilet seat as a natural enemy.

CHLOE. Can we not talk about toilet seats right after breakfast? Thank you. I just hope you're all going to get into that pool—that includes you, too, Sally!—and stay there all weekend. If I weren't allergic to chlorine, you'd never get me out of that thing. Is that a kick in the ass or what?

SAM. So what are we going to do today? What's the agenda?

CHLOE. No agenda. Swim, take a walk, read, volleyball, paint, barbecue, nap, doze, eat, drink, laze, nothing.

SAM. That's a lot, sis. I'm exhausted.

JOHN. What time is it, Chloe?

CHLOE. What do you care what time it is? We're at the beach.

JOHN. What time is it, Sally?

CHLOE. Don't tell him, Sally.

JOHN. Sally?

SAM. It's a little after nine.

JOHN. Thank you. Petal?

    He holds up his empty coffee mug. Chloe takes it from him.

CHLOE. *Oui, mon amour.* One cup of java coming up! Sam? Sally?

SALLY. No, thank you.

CHLOE. Are you sure?

SALLY. Not now, thanks.

CHLOE. It's from Nussbaum's and Claverstock's, their special, special blend.

JOHN. Honey, they don't know about Nussbaum's and Claverstock's.

CHLOE. Well excuse me! I thought everyone knew about Nussbaum's and Claverstock's. It's only been written up in every newspaper and magazine in America. Sam? *Encore du café?*

SAM. You're an angel of mercy! I thought you'd never ask. Of course I could have gotten it myself but I'm the kind of guy who likes to see a woman toil on his behalf.

CHLOE. Did you hear that, Mrs. Truman?

SAM. I'm old-fashioned. So sue me. God, if you weren't my sister I'd jump all over you. You are married to a winner, John, a winner.

CHLOE. Did you tell Dad we were getting together this weekend?

SAM. He wouldn't remember if I did. When are you going down again?

CHLOE. I'm trying for the weekend after Labor Day. I hate that place. The children and John won't go with me anymore.

    Sam and Chloe look out to sea.

SAM. Remind you of something?

CHLOE. What do you think? The 29th St. beach. So where's the roller coaster and the salt water taffy stand?

SAM. Those were the days! Fresh Air Camp.

CHLOE. Oh come on, it wasn't a Fresh Air Camp.

SAM. It was a Fresh Air Camp.

CHLOE. From Asbury Park to this. You've come a long way, baby.

SAM. We both have.

CHLOE. Nussbaum's and Claverstock's is this fabulous gourmet food shop in New Canaan. John hates me to shop there but if you want quality, you have to pay for it, right?

SAM. Sis, this is your kid brother you're talking to. Gourmet to me is a baked potato with sour cream.

CHLOE. Well, married to a woman who doesn't cook.

SAM. Sally cooks.

CHLOE. My lips are sealed. Relax. For the next three days you're in very good hands. *(Pats his stomach.)* When she telephoned, I told Sally I'd take care of everything this weekend. Most women would resent another woman taking over their kitchen.

SAM. It's not really her kitchen yet.

CHLOE. It's the Fourth of July. I'm going to celebrate if it kills me. They've predicted perfect weather for this weekend; I'm going to keep it that way. Gray skies are going to clear up, put on a happy face!

JOHN. Chloe, I thought you were bringing us fresh coffee.

CHLOE. I'm going, I'm going. *J'y vais à la cuisine.* And when I come back I'm going to blow my whistle and I expect everyone to jump into that pool. That goes for you, too, Sally. For the next three days I want you to think of me as your charming, capable pool girl. Oops, oops, oops! Pool *person.* Sorry, Sally.

JOHN. Chloe.

CHLOE. *Je suis dehors d'ici.* I'm outta here! *Fermez la porte!*

SAM. What?

CHLOE. Close the door!

> *Chloe goes through the sliding glass doors into the kitchen, which is just off the deck. We will be able to see her preparing the coffee, even though she is clearly out of earshot. She sings to herself as she works.*

SAM. What's with my sister? She seems unusually hyper, even for her.

JOHN. Really?

SAM. You haven't noticed a change?

JOHN. No, but then I'm married to her.

SAM. It's not the kids?

JOHN. The kids are fine. They're with their grandmother.

CHLOE. *(From the kitchen.)* How does everyone want their coffee?

JOHN. If you don't know after all these years—!

CHLOE. *(Off.)* I was being polite, John.

JOHN. Well don't. This group is beyond polite.

CHLOE. *(At the door.)* Besides, I was speaking to our hosts.

SAM. Oh, come on, Chloe. We're not your hosts. You're family.

CHLOE. Milk, Sam?

SAM. I don't suppose you have any half 'n' half?

CHLOE. I do. Just for you. I know that's how you take it. Sugar?

SAM. Sweet'N Low?

CHLOE. Half a packet?

SAM. More like a third.

CHLOE. Coming up. *(To John.)* See how simple that was, darling?
    She goes back into kitchen.

SAM. You two are okay?

JOHN. We're terrific. We have New England's longest-running, happiest, most fecund shotgun marriage.

SAM. Is that supposed to be funny?

JOHN. Not especially.

SAM. Because it's not.

JOHN. There was no major in comedy at Williams. There should be.

SAM. That's a very annoying habit of yours. Reading while someone is talking to you.

JOHN. I'm not really reading. I'm more like skimming. Besides, I can do both. You think your sister seems a little extra hyper, even by her own high standards, and I'm being told by that book reviewer whose name I can never pronounce that we should all be home reading a new biography of Melville this weekend. Apparently, the whale isn't a metaphor, it's a whale. You have my complete attention, Sam.

John turns the page.

SAM. It's very unpolite.

JOHN. Impolite. I'm sorry.

SAM. I'd like you to stop it.

JOHN. Why?

SAM. I don't like it.

He pulls the paper away from John.

Look at me when I speak to you.

JOHN. All right.

SAM. That's more like it.

JOHN. What do you want to say?

SAM. It's very rude to read while people are speaking to you.

JOHN. I can see that.

SAM. It makes them feel unimportant.

JOHN. That was not my intention.

SAM. Well, that's how it comes across.

He hands paper back to John.

Don't let me interrupt you. I've made my point.

John resumes reading. Sam crosses to Sally painting.

Did you hear all that? I guess that's telling him. Asshole. This is their last weekend. Quick, what's "fecund"? What's the matter?

SALLY. There's someone out there.

SAM. So?

SALLY. Way, way out there. Too far. I don't like it.

SAM. Where?

SALLY. Way, way out there. You can just see his head. There he is! See?

SAM. No.

SALLY. Now the waves are in the way. There!

SAM. I don't see anyone.

SALLY. Just before he swam out, he turned and waved but I don't think it was to me. I thought maybe he was—there! See him?—waving to David, that he hadn't heard, so I waved back, just in case, but it was more like he was waving to the house than to someone in it. It was like a salute or a farewell. Then he walked right into the surf and started swimming straight out, like he was going somewhere. You know, with a purpose. Strong, steady, powerful strokes.

SAM. If he's that kind of swimmer, I don't know what you're worrying about. We'll give him a big hand when he swims in.

SALLY. I've been watching him all morning. I got up early to paint and he was already down there on the beach, as if he'd been there all night. He was sitting with his knees pulled up to his chest, looking out to sea. At one point, he turned and looked up to the house here for a long, long time. Just stared.

SAM. Sure, he heard about your brother and was checking this place out to rob it. Let's make sure people know somebody's here.

SALLY. It was like that scene in that movie.

SAM. What scene, what movie?

SALLY. You know the one.

SAM. There are a million movies, Sally.

SALLY. Help me.

SAM. How should I know? You mangle the name of every one of them. Last Saturday you wanted to rent *Zorro the Greek*.

SALLY. The man swims out.

SAM. What man?

SALLY. I don't know. Gregory Peck!

SAM. Gregory Peck swims out in something? You sure you don't mean Johnny Weissmuller?

SALLY. No! *A Star Was Born*.

SAM. *A Star Was Born* with Gregory Peck?

SALLY. And Judy Garland.

SAM. Jesus, Sally!

SALLY. What did I say?

SAM. You know how this drives me crazy.

SALLY. It wasn't Judy Garland?

SAM. Yes, it was Judy Garland. But it was *A Star Is Born*. *A Star Is Born*. You are the only person on this entire planet who would say *A Star Was Born*. And it was James Mason.

SALLY. Well whoever he was—.

SAM. He was James Mason, for Christ's sake!

SALLY. Well he never came back.

SAM. Of course he never came back. It was a sad movie.

SALLY. I thought it was a musical.

SAM. It was a sad musical. You're pushing all my buttons.

SALLY. There, you can see his robe on the beach where he dropped it.

SAM. We'll keep an eye on it for him.

SALLY. He wasn't wearing anything.

SAM. You mean, he was naked? On a public beach? That's outrageous. Did you hear that, John? There's a guy out there skinny-dipping with women and children around.

JOHN. Very few women and even fewer children.

SAM. Anybody could see him. Sally did. It's against the law. Suppose I wanted to whip my dick out?

JOHN. This is Fire Island, Sam. I would strenuously argue against it.

SAM. That's not funny.

SALLY. He had a beautiful body.

SAM. I'm sure he did. Most of them do. It's one of their require- ments. If I had nothing to do all day but work out in a gym I would, too. Unfortunately, I own a construction company that has a funny way of almost going under every three months. And we all thought you were painting.

He nuzzles Sally from behind.

You're waiting for some strange guy to come out of the water so you can get a look at his whose-y. I'll show him a real whopper the next time he looks up here. Are you going to let me fly you to the moon this weekend? I'm all yours. Now what about this fecund? What does it mean when you say something is fecund?

SALLY. That it's fertile, abundant.

SAM. Oh. That's what I thought it meant.

SALLY. There he is! See him? Way, way, way out. No one should be out that far alone.

Chloe is at the sliding glass door carrying a large tray with the coffee and lots of breakfast cakes and goodies. She has changed outfits.

CHLOE. Yoo-hoo! Come and get it!

SALLY. What if something happens to him?

SAM. Nothing's going to happen to him.

CHLOE. Does somebody want to give me a hand with this door?

Sam goes to Chloe's aid. John lowers his newspaper and looks across the deck to Sally, who continues to stand looking out to sea.

I wasn't going to tempt anyone with more *délices du A&P* but with this salt air, nothing keeps. My buns are positively soggy. Don't look now, but there are signs of life next door. A young man in a red bikini. *Très, très* fetching. I said, don't look now, Sam!

SAM. I'm not looking. Jesus Christ!

CHLOE. Sam!

SAM. Did you see that guy, John?

JOHN. I used to look like that.

CHLOE. In your dreams.

JOHN. Does anybody mind if I do the puzzle?

CHLOE. They'd be too polite to say if they did. Sally, you need a microwave in the kitchen.

SAM. Sally doesn't like microwaves.

CHLOE. How anyone can live without a microwave! Well I guess if you don't have children...! I brought out some more of those chocolate donuts you like.

SAM. Chloe, you are the devil in a...whatever that is you're wearing.

He takes several donuts and muffins from the tray.

CHLOE. You like it?

SAM. *(To Sally.)* Honey, you should have something like this.

CHLOE. It wouldn't suit her. *(To John.)* What can I get you, John?

JOHN. I don't want anything. We just ate.

CHLOE. A bran muffin at least. Just one. I'll toast and butter it for you.

JOHN. I won't eat it.

CHLOE. No one's going to make you, little boy. You can just look at it. *(To Sam.)* You want me to toast that for you, too?

SAM. This is fine.

CHLOE. It's no trouble.

> *She takes a muffin from Sam's plate and heads back into the house.*

I'm toasting a muffin for you, John.

> *No response.*

De rien, monsieur.

> *She stands in front of the sliding glass door.*

Does somebody want to get this door for me?

> *Sam opens it for her.*

Merci, mon frère.

> *She goes into the house.*

Now if you'll be kind enough to close it for me before the beach gnats, sand flies, and other uglies swarm in...!

> *Sam closes the sliding door.*

Merci encore.

> *Again we will watch Chloe working in the kitchen and again we will be able to hear her singing to herself. Chloe is almost never silent. She also almost never stops working.*

SAM. You don't call that hyper?

JOHN. I barely listen anymore, Sam.

SAM. She hasn't shut up since we got here.

JOHN. She's happy to see you.

SAM. Shit!

JOHN. What's the matter?

SAM. That guy in the red bikini is looking down here.

JOHN. Ignore him.

SAM. I'm trying to. He waved at me.

JOHN. So wave back.

SAM. You wave back. Imagine if they thought we were queer. I'm gonna sit with my legs apart and smoke a cigar all weekend. Why do these houses have to be so close together?

JOHN. Beach property is expensive.

SAM. The first thing we're going to do if we keep this place is build a deck higher than theirs. I don't want people looking down on me. Right, honey?

He joins Sally at her easel. John lowers his paper and looks at Sally.

SALLY. I don't see him, Sam.

SAM. He probably swam in while we were talking.

SALLY. His robe's still there.

SAM. I don't know what you're so worried about. Good swimmers like that know what they're doing. Besides, I don't know how you can see anything in this glare. I bet there's a good pair of binoculars around here somewhere. I'm gonna look around.

SALLY. Sam? Why did you ask me about fecund?

SAM. I don't know. I just did. I'll be right back. I bet I find something.

JOHN. Look at me, Sally, I'm right here.

SAM. I'll be right back. I bet I find something.

JOHN. Look at me, Sally. I'm right here.

Sam and John continue this refrain in low, almost inaudible voices.

CHLOE. *(From inside the kitchen.)* Did somebody say something?

SALLY. I don't know whether to tell you I'm pregnant. I've disappointed you so many times. The last one would have been a boy. No, was a boy. He was a boy. You think I'm crazy to find out their sexes. You think it just makes losing them more painful. It probably does for you but I want to know what they would have been. It helps me to believe there's some reason we're having this trouble.

18

CHLOE. *(From inside.)* Did somebody say something?

SAM. I bet I find something. *(Goes to bedroom.)*

JOHN. I'm right here.

SALLY. *(Calling off.)* I will have a muffin, Chloe.

CHLOE. *(From the kitchen.)* Coming right up!

SALLY. No, I'm having this trouble—all by myself. Sam is the fecund one. I can reproduce but I'm unable to deliver them. We only go so far together. I wouldn't want me for a mother either. Too frightened, too sad, too late.

SAM. *(From within.)* Sally! Come here! Look what I found!

SALLY. Sam!

SAM. Can I have another coffee, sis?

CHLOE. *(From within.)* I just poured it. I read your mind.

SALLY. "That's crazy, Sal. Embryos don't think," Sam tells me, stroking my arm, proving he knows something about reproduction but completely missing my point. "It's comforting, Sam. It's a story. It has a beginning, a middle and an end. It has cause and effect, unborn heroes and a villain." I like it. The truth is just too formless to grasp.

SAM. Can I have another coffee, sis?

CHLOE. *(From within.)* I just poured it. I read your mind.

JOHN. I hope to God she can't read mine.

> *He retreats behind his newspaper. Sam enters with a large carton of items from the closet. He gives a pair of binoculars to Sally. He starts rummaging through the carton, taking things out.*

SAM. I hit the jackpot. There's a closet in there filled with all sorts of things.

SALLY. I don't think we should be doing this. I think we should ask Aaron first.

> *During the following exchange, Sam will continue to remove various items from the carton.*

SAM. It's our house now. Everything left is ours. I'm sure all the really good stuff is gone.

SALLY. Aaron wouldn't take anything that wasn't his.

SAM. Don't be so naive.

SALLY. He was my brother's friend.

SAM. He was your brother's boyfriend. I'm sure he took what he wanted. Wake up and smell the coffee.

SALLY. I hate it when you talk like that.

He's found the safety deposit box at the bottom of the carton.

SAM. Double Bingo! Talk like what?

SALLY. I don't want to know any more of my brother's secrets.

SAM. I think you found out the big one a long time ago. I'm going to need something to get in this: a file or a hammer. I'm going to look in that utility shed for a toolbox.

SALLY. Why are you doing this?

SAM. Someone has to.

SALLY. Where are you going?

JOHN. It's under the house.

SALLY. Why are you doing this?

SAM. I know they talk about me. I've never left a room without knowing people talk about me. It's a terrible feeling, I've always had it, it had no beginning, it just was—but I've made my peace with it and I have my revenge. I talk about them. To myself. And I can really tell the truth to myself. Put two people together and truth doesn't stand a chance.

SALLY. Where are you going?

SAM. I'm going to look in that utility shed.

JOHN. I have cancer, Sally.

SAM. I'm going to look in that utility shed.

JOHN. We'll be right here.

SALLY. Just be careful.

SAM. Of what? "Be careful"!

Sam goes.

SALLY. *(Looking at her work.)* How did they do it, the Masters? What did they know I don't?

JOHN. I have cancer, Sally.

SALLY. Oops, I'm sorry. You're trying to read.

JOHN. I have cancer, Sally. It's only a little speck now, a microscopic dot of pain and terror but they tell me it will soon grow and ripen and flower in this fertile bed of malignancy that has somehow become my body. I never meant it to. When it blossoms and when and if they cut it from me, all will marvel at its size, dark beauty and malevolence. They will then take this enormous cancer and give it to a medical university—Johns Hopkins or Cornell—and it will be displayed there in a Cancer Hall of Fame for generations of young doctors, to study and marvel at. No cancer will be worse than mine, Sally, nor none more virulent, more horrendous, more agonizing. I am scared, Sally. I am very, very scared.

SALLY. *(Looking out to sea.)* Whoever you are, my strong, silent, beautiful swimmer, come back safely. Look after him, God. Don't let him drown, even if that was his intention. Don't let him haunt my dreams. Amen.

CHLOE. *(At the sliding glass door with a tray in hand.)* Me voilà! I thought you'd all be in that pool by now.

JOHN. We will, Chloe, we will.

CHLOE. Does somebody want to give me a hand—?

    No one responds.

Sometimes I feel like the Invisible Woman!

    Sally comes to her rescue.

SALLY. I've got it.

CHLOE. This would have been so much quicker with a microwave. So where is Sam the Man?

SALLY. He's under the house.

CHLOE. What's he doing under the house? Your neighbors are very, very attractive.

SALLY. He's snooping.

SAM. *(From below.)* I'm not snooping, I'm exploring!

JOHN. Don't start with the neighbors, Chloe.

CHLOE. Do I look like I'm starting?

JOHN. You always look like you're starting.

CHLOE. I like people. I love you.

> *She kisses John on the top of the head.*

That was wonderful last night. I'm still glowing. "Gigue." Four Down is "gigue."

JOHN. You know I hate it when you do that.

CHLOE. "So sue me. Sue me. Shoot bullets through me." *(She is almost singing it by now.)* "I love you." God, I love that show, it's a classic. *(Waves.)* Good morning!

JOHN. Chloe!

CHLOE. He waved at me first. Who are you anyway? Bluebeard? Henry the Eighth? Someone got up on the wrong side of bed this morning!

> *She joins Sally at her easel.*

I guess that's telling him. I wish I could do that.

SALLY. Why don't you try it?

CHLOE. It's too deep for me. Jazz exercise is about as profound as I want to get. That and Little Theatre. Did you really like me in *A Little Night Music*?

SALLY. Yes.

CHLOE. That Sondheim is such a little devil. He writes real tongue twisters. I don't suppose people like you have ever wanted to get up on a stage and expose themselves?

SALLY. Not really.

CHLOE. Count your blessings. It's a curse. Stick with your painting. Do you ever sell anything?

SALLY. Neighbors, people at the office.

CHLOE. I envy you sometimes. A real job. John says I'm too emotional to work. That's coming along. I'm impressed.

SALLY. I'm not very happy with it. Trying to put the power of all that, the play of light, the volume, the space, onto canvas with a brush and a few colors. It's pathetic. It's arrogant almost.

CHLOE. Well it's not like you're out robbing liquor stores.

SALLY. I think I see the ocean but when I try to break it down into colors, forms, brush strokes, it all comes apart, and I don't think I'm capable of truly understanding or seeing anything at all.

CHLOE. There you go again, Sally. Deep, deep, deep. I thought you did this for fun. You make it sound like torture. That's why I won't do heavy drama. They're doing Arthur Miller next month. "No way," I told them. Listen, I even think a show like *Carousel* is pushing its luck. I love how you do that with the brush, those swirly-swirl-swirls! Does this bother you?

SALLY. Yes.

CHLOE. I'm sorry. *(Calling to Sam.)* Sam? What are you doing down there?

JOHN. Why don't I just get a large rock and bash her head in?

CHLOE. Sam!

SAM. *(From below.)* What?

CHLOE. What are you going to feel like for dinner?

SAM. *(From below.)* I thought I'd throw a shark on the barbie, mate!

JOHN. Jesus, Chloe, we just had breakfast.

CHLOE. That's all that one thinks about, food! He used to drive our poor mother crazy. I don't know how you put up with him, Sally! *(To John.)* Look who wasn't hungry.

JOHN. Shove food in somebody's face and of course they'll eat it.

CHLOE. I didn't shove food in your face. I put a buttered, toasted Entenmann's bran muffin on your plate.

JOHN. You know I have no will power. You married a weak man.

CHLOE. I wish you wouldn't say things like that. It's very upsetting. It's certainly not amusing.

JOHN. It wasn't meant to be.

CHLOE. I think this whole weekend will be fraught enough for Sally without you contributing your very peculiar dark humor. I can take your little barbs. After fourteen years, I'm like an archery target! But I don't think other people understand or appreciate them. 'Nuff said? God, what a glorious day!

Music has begun from next door. The selection is Schubert's

Moments musicaux, no. 3 in F Minor. Chloe breathes it in.

Listen to that! *Crème de la crème,* your neighbors, what did I tell you? I love classical music. It's so soothing. What is this piece, Sally? You know everything.

SALLY. I think it's Schubert. One of the *Moments musicaux.*

CHLOE. You're pretty smart for a girl.

SALLY. I don't know everything, Chloe.

CHLOE. Yes, you do.

> *Chloe goes back into the kitchen. We will be able to watch her take things from the toaster, butter them, etc., and arrange everything on a tray.*

JOHN. Sally, do you know a seven-letter word beginning with "t," ending with "r," that's a coin in the Gabon Republic?

SALLY. What do you think, John?

JOHN. You've never ceased to astonish me.

SALLY. There's always a first time.

JOHN. That's all right, just so long as there's never a last.

CHLOE. *(From the kitchen.)* Did somebody call me?

JOHN. They both know. They have to know. It's in the way we look at each other. It's in the way we don't look at each other. She knows my eyes are on her. Have been all morning. Turn around, Sally. I'm not going to hurt you. Look at me. Please.

SALLY. How many times David must have stood right here and tried to take all this in with his camera. The sea, the sky. It's too much, it's overwhelming. I feel diminished.

JOHN. "Trapkur"!

SALLY. Diminished. That was his word. At Dad's funeral when David was trying to comfort Mom and she said he couldn't really understand her loss, or know what she was feeling, that the love between a man and a woman was different, I should have stood up for David because when Mom said that, he couldn't stand up for himself. I just looked away. Instead of feeling comforted, he told me, he felt rejected and diminished by us both. What a terrible word. Diminished.

JOHN. "Trapkur"!

SALLY. What?

JOHN. It's "trapkur," the word is "trapkur."

SALLY. If you say so!

JOHN. I made it up.

SALLY. Isn't that cheating?

JOHN. I just wanted you to turn around. I had a feeling a word like "trapkur" would do the trick. Hi, Sally, remember me?

SALLY. Yes, John.

CHLOE. *(From the kitchen.)* Sally, may I have a word with you?

SALLY. I'd like to finish this before the light—.

CHLOE. *(At the sliding glass door.)* This could be serious.

SALLY. What, Chloe?

CHLOE. I don't see any Kahlúa.

SALLY. We'll manage.

CHLOE. Maybe we'll manage but we won't be having any Black Russians after supper. I'm doing a total inventory in there for you.

SALLY. That's all right.

CHLOE. I don't mind.

SALLY. I wish you wouldn't.

CHLOE. I have no emotional investment in this house. I only met David once. Is he still down there? Sam?

SAM. *(From below.)* What? They've got a lot of nice things down here!

CHLOE. First call for alcohol. Do you want something?

SAM. *(From below.)* You mean like a drink?

SALLY. Sam!

CHLOE. No, I mean like an enema! Drove her stark, raving mad!

SAM. *(From below.)* What is everyone else having?

JOHN. I'll have a Bloody Mary. Very, very hot.

CHLOE. John's having a Bloody Mary.

SAM. *(From below.)* That sounds great. But not too hot.

CHLOE. I know how you like it. Do I know how he likes it. Sally?

SALLY. Nothing for me. Sam!

SAM. *(From below.)* What?

SALLY. It's only—.

SAM. *(From below.)* What!

SALLY. Nothing.

SAM. *(From below.)* Jesus Christ!

CHLOE. What happened?

SAM. *(From below.)* I just saw a big fucking snake down here.

CHLOE. Well, leave it there! *Je n'aime pas les serpents.*

SALLY. I told you to be careful.

CHLOE. Did he ever put a snake in your bed when you were trying to read a book and it crawled up your leg?

SALLY. Not that I remember, Chloe.

CHLOE. Count your blessings. When we were kids he used to do it all the time. No snakes up here, Sam! Got that?

SAM. *(From below.)* John! Come down and look at this snake!

JOHN. Leave me out of this.

CHLOE. God, it's so beautiful out here I could cry. *Bonjour, tristesse!*

SALLY. Chloe, why do you always sprinkle your conversation with French?

CHLOE. Because I'm bored with English. *(Singing.) Non, rien de rien. Non, je ne regrette rien.*

> She goes into the kitchen and begins making drinks.

JOHN. I'm married to Édith Piaf.

SALLY. She's a very nice woman.

JOHN. I know. Believe me, I know.

SAM. *(From below.)* I think it's a copperhead.

JOHN. Have you thought about what happened?

SALLY. Of course I have.

JOHN. You haven't even looked at me.

SALLY. That's not true.

JOHN. You said you would call.

SALLY. She's right inside.

CHLOE. *(From the kitchen.)* Did you say something, darling?

JOHN. Are you going to be like this all weekend?

SALLY. I knew this would happen.

SAM. *(From below.)* It's too big for a coral snake.

CHLOE. *(From the kitchen.)* There's no Smirnoff. They've got Stoli and Absolut.

SAM. *(From below.)* I'm going to kill it.

> *We hear the sounds of a spade striking the sand from under the house. It will continue for maybe thirty seconds while the action on the deck continues.*

Ugh!

> *John has kissed Sally. She slaps him.*

CHLOE. *(From the kitchen.)* John? The Stoli or the Absolut?

JOHN. The Stoli.

CHLOE. *(From the kitchen.)* What about Sam?

JOHN. The Stoli. We'll all drink Russian vodka and get very Chekhovian.

CHLOE. That sounds like a terrible idea.

SALLY. We'll talk.

JOHN. When?

SALLY. I promise.

JOHN. He follows you around like a dog.

SALLY. That's not true.

JOHN. I've got an erection.

SALLY. Don't say things like that.

CHLOE. *(From the kitchen.)* It's very hard to hear you in here!

SAM. *(From below.)* This is gross! It's all over the shovel.

JOHN. I want you so much. Just let me just hold you.

SALLY. I can't.

JOHN. Please.

SALLY. No.

Chloe appears at the sliding glass door with a tray of drinks.

CHLOE. *Voilà les beverages!*

JOHN. Hold it!

He goes quickly to the door and opens it for her.

CHLOE. I don't believe it. This is one doll you can knock over with a feather. I made Sally a Diet Pepsi, just in case. Sally, I made you a Diet Pepsi, just in case. Sam! If he brings a snake up here! How's your puzzle?

JOHN. Impossible. It's got a theme. I hate theme puzzles.

CHLOE. I can't believe I know someone who can do the *New York Times* crossword in ink without cheating! And that I'm married to him? I'm very impressed with myself.

JOHN. What are you talking about? You got "gigue."

CHLOE. It's a dance term. I've had training. Ask me who wrote *Gone with the Wind* and I draw a blank.

Sam comes back onto the deck from the stairs below. He is carrying a file and a hammer in an open gardener's basket.

Do you have that snake with you?

SAM. Sis, I am a grown man with my own business, two mortgages and a hernia operation next month. I don't have time to play with snakes.

CHLOE. This is just what he used to do: all innocence.

SAM. Where would I have a snake? In here?

He pulls something out that looks very like a dead snake. Chloe screams.

It's a piece of hose for Christ's sake! Do you believe this?

CHLOE. I fall for it every time!

SAM. Here's the snake.

He pulls out a real dead snake and dangles it in front of Chloe, who screams and runs into the house. Then he dangles it in front of Sally, who doesn't flinch.

You're pretty brave for a girl.

SALLY. Married to you I'd have to be. Now get rid of it.

He dangles the snake in front of John, who looks at it calmly.

SAM. John's not scared of snakes. John was in the Peace Corps in darkest Africa.

JOHN. That looks like a pith viper.

SAM. What the hell is a pitch viper?

CHLOE. *(From within.)* Is it gone? I'm not coming out of here until it's gone!

JOHN. *Pith* viper. We had them in Chad. I'm glad you killed it. They're fatal.

SAM. Yeah?

JOHN. You didn't get any venom on you? It can eat right through the skin.

SAM. What do you know? Learn something every day. Fucking Fire Island. They ought to have signs up. Beware of snakes.

CHLOE. *(From within.)* Don't even think about lunch as long as that snake is out there!

> *Sam throws the snake into the beach grass on the side of the house.*

SALLY. Sam!

SAM. What?

SALLY. That's the neighbor's property!

SAM. It's not my snake. We don't own it. It's not like I threw a beer can in their yard. It probably came from under their house anyway. It heard unfamiliar voices and came over to check us out.

SALLY. And got its head bashed in for its trouble.

SAM. Whose side are you on? The snake's?

SALLY. I don't know why you have to kill everything.

SAM. I don't kill everything. That's a lousy thing to say. I don't kill everything.

> *He goes into their room to wash his hands.*

SALLY. I didn't mean that. He gets me so—!

JOHN. I know. *(Calling off.)* It's okay, Petal!

SALLY. What's the word I want?

29

Chloe comes out on the deck.

CHLOE. Is the coast clear?

SALLY. Angry.

JOHN. I know. All clear!

SALLY. I'm sorry, Chloe.

CHLOE. Don't. It's brother-sister stuff. If he'd done it to you or John it would have been hostile. Where is the son of a bitch?

SALLY. I think he's washing his hands.

SAM. *(From within.)* I'm washing my hands!

> *Music begins from the house on the left of them. A bluesy morning-after ballad sung by a bluesy morning-after female singer.*

JOHN. Oh, great! Now we've got stereo. Are you okay, Petal?

CHLOE. I'm fine. How are you?

> *Sam comes out of their room, drying his hands.*

SAM. I'm sorry, sis. It was just a joke.

CHLOE. Remind me to laugh when I get home from Bellevue after I've had a complete nervous breakdown.

> *We hear a recording of the Queen of the Night's aria from Mozart's* The Magic Flute *being loudly played in one of the adjacent beach houses.*

SAM. That's another real toe-tapper.

JOHN. I thought people went to the beach for peace and quiet. I hope those are renters, Sally. You don't want permanent neighbors like that.

SAM. You want me to go over and say something to them, honey? You know, tell them who we are. The new owners.

SALLY. I think they know.

JOHN. *(Calling off.)* Excuse me! Excuse me! Gentlemen! Would you mind turning that down, thank you!

CHLOE. Party pooper!

JOHN. *(Low.)* Goddamn fairies.

CHLOE. We didn't hear that. *(To others.)* He doesn't mean it. We have three gay men and one lesbian in administration at Sturman. God only knows how many on faculty. One of the men in admissions right under John has AIDS. John has been terrific about it.

JOHN. Shut up, Chloe.

SAM. John.

CHLOE. It's all right. I need it. I want it, in fact. I tend to run on. John keeps me in line.

She kisses John on the top of the head.

He's my knight in shining armor!

JOHN. Chloe, you know I hate it when you do that.

CHLOE. So spank me, daddy. Spank me right out here in total daylight. *(To Sam and Sally.)* You know, I'm not usually like this. You know what this is? It's being without the kids. It's grown-up time. We can behave like grown-ups! Fuck, fuck, fuck. Shit, shit, shit. Piss, piss, piss. Cunt, cunt, cunt. Dick, dick, dick.

SAM. Have you taken your medication, Chloe?

CHLOE. One day people are going to believe you when you say things like that. I'm not on medication, Sally. I hope nobody minds if I shut up for a while. I'm gonna get some sun.

Chloe puts down a blanket and applies lotion to her legs. Sam pushes the locked box aside and comes over to where Sally is painting.

SAM. I'm losing my touch. I was famous where I grew up for picking locks. I could hot-wire any car in thirty seconds flat, even a Mercedes. I seriously considered a life of crime but then I met you and went straight. I like that.

SALLY. Thank you.

SAM. I really like that.

SALLY. This is the part I hate most about painting: people looking at it. They're not looking, they're judging and it's never as good as I want it to be but it's always better than anyone thinks it is. Humble-slash-arrogant. That's me.

SAM. My brain has become a collision course of random thoughts. Some trivial, but some well worth the wonder. Sometimes I think I'm losing my mind. I'm not sure of anything anymore. It's the same anxiety I have when I think I've forgotten how to tie my tie or tie my shoelaces or I've forgotten how to swallow my food and I'm going to choke on it. Three days ago I was standing in front of our bathroom mirror in terror because I couldn't knot my tie. I wanted to say "Sally, please come in here and help me." But I couldn't. What would she have thought? Last night I spit a piece of steak into my napkin, rather than risk swallowing it because I was afraid I would choke. Maybe it's trivial and that's why no one wants to talk about it, so I'm talking to myself. No one wants to listen to who we really are. Know somebody really. Know you leave shit stains in your underwear and pick your nose. Tell a woman you've forgotten how to swallow your food and she's in her car and out of your life before you can say "Wait, there's more. Sometimes I have to think about someone else when I'm with you because I'm afraid I won't stay hard if I don't. Or how much I want to fuck the teenage daughter of the couple that lives three doors down. How my father takes all the air out of the room and I can't breathe when I'm with him. How if I could tear my breast open and rip out my heart and feed it to these seagulls in little raw pieces, that pain would be nothing to the one I already feel, the pain of your betrayal! How most afraid I am of losing you." How can I tell you these things and there be love?

SALLY. —slash-arrogant. That's me.

SAM. Well, I really like it.

Sally has seen something on the beach below and in front of the deck.

SALLY. Hey! Hey! I see you! I see what you're doing!

SAM. What's happening?

SALLY. That's not his robe. He's taking that guy's robe. That's not your robe! I know who it belongs to!

CHLOE. John! Trouble!

John gets out of the chaise.

SALLY. We have witnesses! We all see you!

SAM. He can't hear you.

SALLY. I'm going to tell him!

SAM. Stay out of it, Sally.

CHLOE. I don't know what the world is coming to.

SALLY. Once upon a time I would have run down there and wrestled someone for doing that. I would have won, too. God, every single day for the rest of my life, with Your help, I want to renew my membership in the human race. Amen. Thank You.

> *John returns to his place on the chaise and reads. Sam takes a hard swing at the lock with the hammer. It falls open but it's broken. He won't be able to re-lock it.*

SAM. Shit!

SALLY. What happened?

SAM. I broke the lock.

SALLY. What are you going to find in there?

SAM. I don't know. What are you so afraid of? Now what have we got here?

CHLOE. Sally?

SALLY. What?

CHLOE. Do you see what I see?

SALLY. Where?

CHLOE. There, on the beach, in the blue thong bikini. Joan Rivers was right about those things. It does look like he's flossing his ass. He's looking up here. Wave.

> *Chloe waves wildly.*

SALLY. Chloe!

CHLOE. All right, don't wave. *(Calling.)* You are so fucking hot, honey!

> *She watches the man disappear.*

You compare that or your brother or your neighbors next door with the hi-fi to our two and you have to ask yourself something: Don't straight men think we have eyes? Don't they occasionally look at themselves in the mirror? God knows, they expect us to. *(To John.)* Give me twenty push-ups. Let's go. The party's over. *(To Sally.)* Sally, can I say something, just woman to woman?

SALLY. Chloe, I don't think I can take any more of your bombshells.

CHLOE. My what?

SALLY. I'm very fragile this weekend. I'm sorry. I adore you, Chloe.

CHLOE. Really?

SALLY. You know I do.

CHLOE. Then say it again. Ever since I turned thirty I've become very needy.

SAM. You were just forty.

CHLOE. I know. Now I'm out of control. If my husband doesn't make love to me this weekend, my own brother isn't safe.

JOHN. We made love last night.

CHLOE. You know what I mean, big love! Last night was *petit*. I'm talking *l'amour grand*! Get out the whips and chains, handcuff me to the bed, let me take a dildo to you and you see what it feels like.

SALLY. This is just what I was talking about.

CHLOE. You and Sam don't have a dildo?

SALLY. No, and even if we did, it's none of your business. I don't enjoy standing on a sundeck in broad daylight on the Fourth of July talking about dildos. I don't think this is what Thomas Jefferson had in mind.

CHLOE. I used to be like that.

SALLY. Like what?

CHLOE. Uptight. Honey, this is Fire Island, not Palm Beach.

> *Music from the house on the left. A very loud, very classic overture to a classic Broadway musical is heard from the house next door. Annie's, of course, would kill the joke.* *

Wait! Stop! Hold everything! We did this show. I know it. It's on the tip of my brain.

JOHN. I come to the shore to hear the ocean, not this noise.

CHLOE. It's not noise, it's theatre music. Come on, John, help me. Name Broadway musicals. Sally!

SAM. You stay out of this. Did I tell you what she hit me with last week? *What's Up Baby Joan!*

SALLY. I still don't see what's wrong with it.

---

* See Special Note on Songs/Recordings at the back of this volume.

SAM. There's no such movie. It's *Whatever Happened to Baby Jane*. *What's Up Doc?* Joan has nothing to do with it.

JOHN. I'm going inside if this keeps up.

CHLOE. I've got it. *Annie*. It's the overture to *Annie*. No wonder I didn't recognize it. I wasn't in *Annie*. I was in Bridgeport General having Megan when we did *Annie*.

SAM. Oh my God, that *Annie*. I cried my eyes out. All those orphans. What a movie.

CHLOE. I didn't see the film version. I generally don't. I'm sure they made many changes unfaithful to the stage production. Hollywood will do that.

> *John gets up and goes into his room. We will be able to see him lie down on the bed and read.*

John, where are you going? We're sorry. We'll stop. *(Calling across to the house on the right.)* Excuse me! My husband isn't feeling well—. Thank you. No, you don't have to turn it all the way off.

> *The volume of the music from the house on the left is lowered before she can call over.*

Thank you! You read our minds!

> *She heads towards their room.*

Darling, they've turned it down. Did you take your—?

JOHN. Yes, Mother.

CHLOE. Would you like a massage?

> *She goes into their room. We can see them sitting on the bed together. After a while we will see Chloe giving John a massage.*

SAM. I'm sorry. It was a bad idea. We shouldn't have done this. I just didn't think we wanted to spend a long weekend together in a strange beach house. I didn't know what we'd be getting into out here.

SALLY. They could have brought the children.

SAM. Any place but this and they probably would have. They're going through a patch. I should talk! We're going through a patch. Every marriage does. As long as there's no one else, we'll work it out.

> *Pause.*

I said, as long as there's no one else, we'll work it out.

SALLY. I heard you.

SAM. Is there someone else?

SALLY. *(After another pause.)* No.

SAM. Then we'll work it out. Weren't you going to see Sugarman this week?

> *Sally nods.*

What did he say?

SALLY. No.

SAM. Have you been—?

SALLY. Yes, everything he tells me to do.

SAM. I'm not—.

SALLY. I didn't say you were.

SAM. It's nobody's fault.

SALLY. Yes, it is.

> *There is a pause. Sam continues to look in the safety deposit box.*

SAM. I found the Certificate of Occupancy the lawyer asked for.

SALLY. I'm leaving all that up to you.

SAM. You act like you're angry David left you this place. Angry or guilty.

SALLY. Sometimes I think I'm a little of both.

SAM. Here's some old photos. This must be when David bought this place. See? There's no pool yet. Here's one of your father standing in front of that stupid old Pontiac he loved.

SALLY. That was just before Dad died.

SAM. What else? Some letters, documents, jewelry, cuff links, a ring…oops!

> *The ring rolls into the pool.*

SALLY. Sam!

SAM. I'll get it.

> *Sally looks into the pool.*

SALLY. It's his ring.

SAM. Where's it going to go? I said I'll get it.

SALLY. I don't see it.

Music has begun during this from the house on the left. "Che puro ciel" from Gluck's Orfeo. *John comes out onto the deck.*

JOHN. Your sister has magic fingers, Sam. She's all yours.

SAM. No, thanks.

JOHN. It's getting hot out here. This is a little more like it. This is beautiful. Do you know what it is, Sally?

SALLY. I think it's by Gluck.

CHLOE. *(From within.)* John?

JOHN. It's very soothing. I feel like I'm floating on a cloud.

SALLY. You should be. It's a description of Paradise. Where the Happy Shades go.

JOHN. Well that's us.

He stretches out on the chaise again.

CHLOE. *(From within.)* Are you coming back, John?

JOHN. Gluck, you say?

SALLY. I'm pretty sure.

SAM. Gluck? Gluck who? Who's Gluck? Where do you know about Gluck from?

JOHN. That's what I want to be! A happy Happy Shade!

SALLY. That's the man I slept with. There! Right there! For just an instant I caught a glimpse of him again.

Chloe comes out on the deck.

CHLOE. I'll do refills.

She goes into the kitchen.

SAM. *(Starts to read from a postcard.)* Here's a postcard from Aaron. "Dear David, Having a terrible time, wish *I* wasn't here." Houston? I don't blame him.

JOHN. Sam?

SAM. What?

JOHN. Sssshhhh. We're blissing out.

SAM. Speak for yourself. I'm too sensitive, that's my problem.

Sally stands and looks out to the ocean.

SALLY. I think I see—! There! Please, God, let it be him!

She stares at the horizon line, not moving now. Sam continues to read, his lips still moving. Chloe is the only one still animated. She is at the sliding screen door with her tray of drinks.

CHLOE. *(From within.)* Don't worry everybody. I can manage this time.

She struggles to open the door with her foot.

Oh!!

She drops the tray. Everything shatters. She is still behind the sliding screen door. She calls out to the others on the deck.

It's all right. Don't get up. I'll handle it.

She begins to clean up. As she works, her movements become slower and slower until she is still. Lights fade down except for special lamps on our four characters. They are isolated by them. They do not move. The Gluck continues to the end of the piece. There is a brief pause. We hear the ocean, maybe a gull. The lights snap off.

End of Act One

ACT TWO

Noon. The sun is beating down on the deck full-strength.

There is music coming from the two houses off. From the stage left house, we hear the first movement of Brahms' Piano Concerto No. 1. From the stage right house, some zydeco.

Sally sits on the edge of the pool, dangling her feet in the water. Her easel stands where she left it. Chloe is cooking hamburgers on the grill. The necessary garnishes are on the picnic table. She has changed into another attractive ensemble.

John is flying a kite, which involves a lot of footwork and bobbing back and forth. Sam has found an astronomical telescope in the locked room and is checking it out.

SALLY. We should do something.

JOHN. Like what?

SALLY. Report it.

JOHN. What are we going to report? Some stranger went swimming and we didn't see him come back?

CHLOE. How does everyone like their burgers?

SALLY. I know he's still out there.

JOHN. If he is, he's drowned and he'll wash up miles from here. Have you ever seen a drowned person? You don't want to. Let it go, Sally.

CHLOE. Sally?

SALLY. Medium rare. This is going to bother me all weekend.

CHLOE. Sam?

SAM. Rare. Very, very rare. *(Fiddling with telescope.)* This is fantastic. Wait until tonight. Does anybody remember if there's a moon?

CHLOE. John? There was a moon last night, almost full.

JOHN. Medium rare. Fly, baby, fly! All right!

He's like one of his students.

SAM. There was a moon last night?

SALLY. Only that big!

SAM. I'm a city boy. Nature kind of rolls off my back. Really, really rare, sis. Bloody.

CHLOE. I know. I've only been cooking burgers for him since he was that high. I'd say "Everybody into that glorious pool," except we're about to eat.

SALLY. Maybe we could call the Coast Guard.

SAM. John's right, Sally. If the guy is drowned, he's drowned. There's nothing we can do about it. If he's not, he's not. And there's still nothing we can do about it. *Que sera, sera.*

SALLY. Am I crazy?

SAM. Yes, you're crazy.

JOHN. Look, it's a speck now!

CHLOE. Of all things to be allergic to! And I love to swim. John calls me a human porpoise.

JOHN. It wasn't a compliment.

CHLOE. I'm taking it as one. I feel about ten years old in the water. The years just come tumbling off and I'm a little girl again. John says he's never seen me happier than that week we went to the islands. Where were we, honey, what island?

JOHN. I don't remember.

SAM. St. Bart's. You sent us a card.

CHLOE. Well, wherever it was—

SAM. It was St. Bart's! Jesus.

CHLOE. Yours truly was in the water from sunup to sundown and then some. We did some skinny-dipping right in front of the hotel.

SAM. At night?

CHLOE. No, in broad daylight! Talk about romantic! I remembered why I married this crazy lug. We started making love right then and there. The moon and stars were shining. The water looked and felt like black velvet.

SALLY. Shut up, please, shut up, all of you.

CHLOE. Yachts were floating, bobbing all around us.

SALLY. Why do people have to speak to one another? Why can't we just be?

CHLOE. Unfortunately, just as you-know-who was getting ready to climax…

She nods with her head toward John flying his kite.

SALLY. David, are you laughing somewhere? I hope so.

CHLOE. …we sort of floated, bobbed ourselves into another couple who were doing exactly the same thing. I wish you could have heard the yell this one let out. The hotel lit up like that.

JOHN. She exaggerates.

CHLOE. People came out of the hotel and onto the boat pier to see what was happening.

JOHN. One person.

CHLOE. We hid behind a little dinghy. "Petal." I'll always remember its name, "Petal."

SAM. "Petal," so that's where he gets it from. I'll say one thing for John. When he wants to, he can be wonderful with her. "Petal." I like that, "Petal." I don't have a name for Sally. Sally doesn't have a name for me.

CHLOE. Funny, the things we remember; the things we don't. Forget the name of the island, remember the name of the boat!

SAM. St. Bart's, for Christ's sake.

CHLOE. How did you say you wanted your burger, Sally?

SALLY. Medium's fine.

SAM. Very rare for me.

JOHN. Medium rare. Look, look at that crazy gull! He's attacking the kite!

Sam and Chloe look up at the kite high above them. Sally just dangles her legs in the water.

SAM. I wish somebody would tell me why we can't eat seagulls. We eat everything else. They're big, they're plentiful. How bad could they be? You could feed a lot of poor people with seagulls. Same with pigeons. There's a lot of meat on your city pigeon.

CHLOE. Just don't go vegetarian on me.

SAM. She knows. She brings one bean sprout into that house and I'm out of there.

CHLOE. Pammie Bernstein went vegetarian and completely lost her singing voice. You're going to lose that kite.

SAM. Pammie Bernstein? I don't think we know her.

CHLOE. Sure you do. *The Pajama Game*, "Steam Heat." She had dink! dink! steam heat. She had dink! dink! steam heat.

SAM. That one? She was terrific. She lost her voice?

CHLOE. Can't get above a middle G now. She doesn't think it's from going vegetarian but I know it is. What else could it be?

JOHN. Hah! Did you see that maneuver? The Red Baron flies again!

SAM. Can I try it awhile?

JOHN. No.

SAM. No?

JOHN. Get your own kite.

SAM. That was the only one in there.

JOHN. Then you should have put it up.

SAM. I didn't know it would be so much fun.

JOHN. Monkey see, monkey do.

SAM. Just for a few minutes.

JOHN. No!

SAM. Please!

JOHN. When I'm done.

SAM. When will that be?

JOHN. When I'm done. Jesus!

SAM. Pig. Kite hog!

SALLY. Sam!

She motions him to join her sitting at the edge of the pool.

CHLOE. If you decide to keep this place, may I make one more teeny-tiny suggestion?

SAM. *(To Sally.)* This is their first and last weekend.

He sits at pool's edge next to Sally.

SALLY. Are you burning? Let me see.

She looks at his neck.

SAM. Ouch! Jesus Christ!

SALLY. Does it hurt?

SAM. It does now. It was fine until you—!

CHLOE. I would landscape like crazsy. I don't care who your neighbors are—Nelson Rockefeller or Nelson Mandela—you don't want them looking at you all day. People stare. It's human nature. Don't get too lovey-dovey comfy down there, you two. We're about to eat.

JOHN. I don't want mine if it's too done.

CHLOE. Go fly a kite!

She breaks herself up.

Well, I thought it was funny.

SALLY. I told you to put sunblock on the back of your neck.

SAM. I hate him.

SALLY. This is what happened in Florida.

Sally will apply a sun lotion to the back of Sam's neck.

SAM. He thinks he's such hot shit because he's the director of admissions at a swanky prep school and they're members of a fucking country club! Ow, I said!

SALLY. I didn't get it all!

SAM. I know you've slept with him.

SALLY. Sam!

SAM. I do.

CHLOE. Come and get it!

SAM. Do you deny it?

CHLOE. *Allons enfants de la Patrie! À table!*

SAM. What's the pause for?

SALLY. That you'd even think such a thing.

CHLOE. Sally? Sam? Earth to Mars. Come in Mars.

SAM. Then you deny it?

43

SALLY. Yes.

SAM. Liar.

Sam gets up from edge of pool and starts putting fixings on his hamburger.

CHLOE. Well I'm glad someone heard me. *(To John.)* You want to bring that in, Captain Lindbergh?

JOHN. Honey, I can eat and—.

CHLOE. No!

JOHN. —do this at the same time.

CHLOE. No! Sometimes I have to put my foot down and this is one of them. We are eating at the table like civilized people.

JOHN. Yes, mother.

He will tie the kite string to his end of the picnic table.

CHLOE. Treat them like adults and you might as well be talking to yourself. But treat them like little boys and *voilà!* Am I right, Sally? Sally knows I'm right. Married to you, she'd have to be.

John and Sam are sitting at the picnic table. Sally is still sitting by the edge of the pool. Chloe is bustling about, serving.

SALLY. It's gone, that moment to speak the truth. He'll ask again, I'll lie again. The truth is, I don't want him to know.

CHLOE. Are you going to be staring at that string all through lunch?

JOHN. Don't let it bother you.

CHLOE. What I do for love! Beautiful song. It should be my anthem. You didn't see it when we did *A Chorus Line*?

SAM. I don't remember.

CHLOE. That's all right, I wasn't in it. Sally, *à table, s'il vous plaît? Merci.* They brought in some director from the city who said she wanted real dancers, whatever that means. Gloria Munster cracked on the high note in that song every single performance, every one. I know. I was ushering. And to show her legs in public on a stage gives new meaning to an old Jewish expression: *chutzpah.*

JOHN. Chloe.

CHLOE. I know: Shut up. Sometimes I can read his mind. Sometimes?!

44

She kisses the top of his head and hugs him from behind.

I can imagine only one thing worse than being married to this man and that is not being married to this man!

She waves to someone on the deck of the next house.

Hi!

Sam and John turn to see whom she is talking to.

What? ...Well, let's hope it *is* good. You can't eat looks! ...I said, you can't eat looks!

JOHN. Sit down, Chloe.

CHLOE. *(Continuing.)* No, no, no! I'm just a friend of the family. *This is David's sister.

Sally waves.

This is her husband, Sam.

Sam waves.

SAM. Why are you doing this?

CHLOE. *(Continuing.)* I'm the overbearing sister-in-law and this is my husband, John.

SAM. Just sit down. Jesus, she's got a whole deckful of them looking at us now.

CHLOE. *(Continuing.)* Who? Aaron? I don't know. *(To Sally.)* Is Aaron coming out?

Sally shakes her head.

No! ...Thank you. You enjoy *yours*. Nice talking to you... What's your name? ...Nice talking to you, Mr. Beckenstein...Harry! *Ciao!*

She sits.

He said to enjoy our lunch.

SAM. Why did you do that?

CHLOE. Do what?

SAM. They're going to think we want to be friends. They'll be over here all the time now. Drinks, barbecues, before you know it, you-know-what.

CHLOE. Because you're such an *homme fatal*!

SAM. What's an *homme fatal*? Something insulting, I bet.

CHLOE. The opposite of a *femme fatale*.

SAM. That's Sally over there.

CHLOE. Sally, it's getting cold.

SALLY. Okay.

She gets up and joins them at the picnic table.

CHLOE. Another teensy suggestion, Sal. Get a gas grill. No more struggling with charcoal, you can control the heat, fabulous!

JOHN. What *are* you thinking about the house?

SALLY. I don't know. It's so far for us. I don't know how much we'd use it. Part of me thinks I should just give it to Aaron.

SAM. The insane-menopausal-crazy-woman part! Minimum, *minimum*, this place is worth eight.

CHLOE. Eight thousand dollars?

SAM. Eight hundred thousand dollars.

CHLOE. That's what I thought. You can't get a closet for eight thousand dollars anymore.

JOHN. Chloe. Why would you give something worth maybe close to a million dollars to a total stranger?

SALLY. He's not a total stranger.

SAM. He's black, y'know.

SALLY. He was wonderful to David. He took extraordinary care of him. Never left his side, slept in the hospital, everything one person can possibly do for another.

SAM. Did you both know he was black? Black, black. Very African, that kind of black. Nothing white about him.

SALLY. There should be some way to acknowledge that kind of devotion.

SAM. I agree. Thank you. Thank you very much. You want the TV set? The books, the records. Take what you want. But an eight-hundred-thousand-dollar beach house? I'm sorry.

SALLY. I keep thinking David would want me to give it to Aaron.

SAM. Then why did he leave it to you?

SALLY. I don't know. I really don't know.

SAM. He got the apartment for Christ's sake.

SALLY. I don't think we'd ever feel really comfortable here.

CHLOE. John?

She motions that he's got catsup on his chin.

SALLY. I don't think I have anything against gay men. I just don't want to be the only non-gay people here.

CHLOE. You don't want to be a token anything. I hear you. Who wants to feel everyone's staring at them?

JOHN. You want my advice? Hang on to it. Property like this is only going to go up in value. There's no shoreline left, from Maine to Florida. It's all been developed. There's no more where this came from. Ten years from now it will be worth two million.

CHLOE. John has a nose for real estate.

JOHN. If you're really uncomfortable here, rent. But hold on to it.

CHLOE. I'm totally comfortable here but then of course I'm in the theatre. Lesbians make me a little nervous but I've never had a problem with the men.

JOHN. Chloe. *(To Sally.)* As far as his friend goes, I wouldn't confuse sentimentality with common sense. I don't know what your finances are like—

SAM. We're doing fine! We're doing fine.

JOHN. —but I can't imagine anyone in this day and age blithely turning their back on eight hundred thousand dollars.

SAM. No one's blithely doing anything, John.

SALLY. Can we not talk about this?

JOHN. I'm sorry I brought it up.

SALLY. Thank you for the advice. Catsup?

CHLOE. Cal and Rhea Kaufman have a place in Vermont and they're always complaining they never get up there. Distance *is* a factor.

SALLY. May I have the catsup, John?

CHLOE. This place would be a hop, skip and a jump for us—we just ferried right across the Sound—

SALLY. Thank you. Relish.

CHLOE. —but for you two! You can have that New Jersey Turnpike. Nothing but trailer trucks! And those signs everywhere: Welcome to the Garden State. What garden? I never saw any garden. I saw refineries and some very unattractive people waiting in line to use the ladies' room at Howard Johnson's.

JOHN. Chloe.

CHLOE. I know. "Shut up." He loves me!

JOHN. This is more than shut up. This is more like a total ban on all sounds emanating from your throat for the next six hours. Let's see. It is now 1:30 P.M. I don't want to hear so much as a peep out of you until 7:30.

SALLY. I'm really not enjoying this, you two.

CHLOE. Oh! It's just us!

SALLY. Well it's very depressing.

CHLOE. Not everyone has your perfect marriage, Sally.

SALLY. I never said it was perfect.

SAM. Try to take it easy, John. She is my sister.

JOHN. Stay out of this.

CHLOE. He's right, Sam. But before I go into my six-hour exile (joyfully! I'll get the second act down pat), I think you should know something about me. All of you. I think it is precisely the small things I run on about and that seem to annoy you so, the little day-to-day details, the nuances, that give our lives some zip and some meaning. I care about cooking the burgers so each of you get exactly what you ask for. I worry about who's driving the children's carpool that particular week. I notice what's going on around me, every detail. I don't miss a thing. I've got all your numbers. I talk too much probably because it's too horrible to think about what's really going on. You should try it, Miss Broody-Woody, Miss High-Falutin! You think you're so superior. Well maybe you are. But to whom? Me? Honey, just about anyone is superior to me. You're going to have to do a lot better than that if you want to keep that attitude up. I'll try to think of something lofty to say at dinner.

She starts to go to her room, then turns back.

You know, I'm not mad at any of you. Really. I think we're all pathetic. Sally, will you clean up? We'll have bugs galore. Pussy Galore! Remember her?

She goes into her room and lies down on her bed.

SAM. One of us should go in there.

JOHN. Why?

SAM. To find out what's wrong.

JOHN. She just told us.

SAM. When did you two get like this?

JOHN. We're fine. We're copacetic, which is the word I'm looking for, Forty-seven Down. Thank you, Sam.

He takes up puzzle.

SAM. I don't think you're so fine.

SALLY. Sam, you heard Chloe. It's none of your business.

SAM. She's my sister.

JOHN. And I'm her husband.

SAM. I love it when you get macho. Especially in that outfit. I start wetting my pants.

JOHN. I'm not going to sit here and exchange puerile insults with my brother-in-law.

SAM. "Puerile"? What's "puerile"?

JOHN. How you're behaving. Look at you!

SAM. I'll show you puerile. Come on, you miserable son of a bitch. You want puerile? You got puerile.

He puts his fists up and starts bobbing back and forth on his feet.

JOHN. Sally, can't you control him?

SALLY. Sam, stop it. I think you're both impossible.

SAM. He wants puerile. Okay, here's some puerile.

He punches John on the arm.

You want more puerile? Okay, here's more puerile.

He keeps punching John on the arm. John slowly stands, which makes Sam dance a little away but still within range.

49

John is clearly making ready to fight.

SALLY. Chloe! Will you come out here?

CHLOE. *(From within.)* There's more beef patties in the refrigerator!

SALLY. Now, Chloe!

JOHN. Look, you little jerk!

SAM. I'm trembling, I'm quaking!

SALLY. Stop it, both of you! Chloe, will you stop them before they hurt one another?

Chloe has come to the door of her room.

CHLOE. Stop them? Honey, I want the cable rights to this.

Sally grabs hold of Sam's arm. He pulls violently away, the force of his gesture sending her reeling.

SAM. I'm going to fucking kill you.

CHLOE. All right, that's enough. Break it up. Both of you!

JOHN. You miserable little asshole.

By now we should realize the men are deadly serious.

CHLOE. John, people are looking from the other deck.

She waves.

Will you gentlemen please tell them how silly they look?

John and Sam keep circling each other, dukes up. Punches have been thrown, but none landed.

JOHN. Come on, big shot. You started something, now let's finish it.

John swings at Sam and misses. Sam swings at John and misses.

SALLY. Sam, you're going to hurt yourself.

SAM. I'll kill the bastard.

CHLOE. Don't rip his shirt, Sam. I just bought it—.

JOHN. Fight fair.

Sally picks up Chloe's large glass container for making sun tea.

SALLY. Okay, that's it!

Sally throws the container of tea at them. It drenches both men but instead of parting them, they leap at each other and start grappling.

SAM. Ow!

John twists Sam's arm behind him in a hammerlock. Now both women rush at them and try to pull them apart.

JOHN. You give up?

SAM. No!

SALLY. You're hurting him, John!

JOHN. You give up?

SAM. No!

JOHN. You give up?

SAM. Yes.

SALLY. Now let him go.

JOHN. "I give up, John."

CHLOE. That's enough, John.

JOHN. "I give up, John!!"

SAM. I give up, John.

SALLY. Now let him go!

She pulls at John.

JOHN. "And I admit I'm a stupid piece of shit."

CHLOE. John, stop it!

Both women are pulling at John now, trying to get him off Sam.

JOHN. "And I admit I'm a stupid piece of shit!!"

SAM. No.

JOHN. "And I admit I'm a stupid piece of shit."

SAM. No.

JOHN. Say it, goddamnit!

SAM. No, I said!

JOHN. Say it!

SAM. No!

JOHN. Say it!!

SAM. No!! Break my fucking arm!

John is suddenly aware of how far his passions have carried him. It is a moment of terrible humiliation for both men. John is now very ashamed of himself.

JOHN. I'm sorry, Sam. I don't know what else to say. I'm sorry. Excuse me.

He goes quickly into his bedroom and throws himself on the bed, his back to the door. Sally and Chloe are helping Sam.

SALLY. Honey, here, lean on me.

CHLOE. Careful.

SAM. I'm fine.

SALLY. Take his other arm.

SAM. Ow!

SALLY. Not that arm.

CHLOE. This arm?

SAM. Ow! Jesus, what are you two? Nurses of pain? I'm fine. Just let go of me.

SALLY. Sit. No, lie down on the chaise. Chloe, get him some ice tea.

SAM. I don't want ice tea.

CHLOE. Good, 'cause there is none. She drenched you in it.

SALLY. What happened? One minute you're horsing around and the next you're trying to kill one another!

CHLOE. Are they still looking over here? I'm too embarrassed to look.

SALLY. You want to lie back? You want to lean forward? Yes? No?

SAM. You're married to a goddamn maniac.

SALLY. Where does it hurt? Tell me.

CHLOE. *(Calling off.)* They were just fooling around. Rehearsing for a play... What? What play? *(To Sally.)* Quick, give me the name of a play, someone.

SALLY. Not now, Chloe.

CHLOE. *(Trying to think.)* Something with violence. Fucking

Alzheimer's! All I can think of is *Bells Are Ringing* and *Bye Bye Birdie. (She's got it.) West Side Story!* They were rehearsing *West Side Story! (Under her breath.)* "Sure they were," they're all going. "Sure they were." I'm so embarrassed!

SALLY. Chloe, believe it or not, but this is not about you and how you feel.

CHLOE. I know that! I was concerned for you. They're your neighbors. You're going to have to live with them. I can stand anything but being misunderstood.

> *She bursts into tears and goes into her room and throws herself on the other bed.*

Why does she hate me? Why does everybody hate me?

SALLY. How do you feel?

SAM. Great. I could bowl ten frames.

SALLY. What happened?

SAM. What do you think? You were right there. He insulted my sister, he insulted me. He's so superior in his pink slacks, his little polo-player shirt and his faggy white shoes. He looks like one of them. He fits right in. You know, we could drive a bigger car, too. We just don't need one. I don't need a BMW to make me feel like I'm somebody. You know what kind of mileage they must get? And I'll tell you something else: I wouldn't want to join any country club that would let him be a member.

> *Sally gives him a big hug.*

What was that for?

SALLY. I love you.

SAM. Thank you. I still hate him.

SALLY. Ssshhh!

SAM. And have you noticed how he holds his fork? Watch him next time. I'm not saying my sister married a fruitcake but she didn't marry any Pete Rose either.

SALLY. Listen to the waves.

SAM. I hate waves. I hate the beach. I hate nature. I like New Jersey.

SALLY. Listen, will you?

A stirring, heroic tenor is heard singing "O Paradis" from the opera L'Africaine *by Meyerbeer.*

It's beautiful.

SAM. Tell me something, what have these people got against Tony Bennett?

SALLY. Every time you say "these people," or "fag" or—you know all the words—I feel I'm holding a stranger.

SAM. I'm sorry, you're right.

SALLY. I don't think they have anything against Tony Bennett. I don't think anybody does. It's all just music.

During this last exchange between Sally and Sam, ever since we became aware of the music, John has gotten up, come out of the bedroom, and walked across the deck to stand at the apron of the stage, facing us. Chloe is still lying on the other bed, Sally and Sam remain rapt in themselves.

JOHN. The weekend's ruined. The four of us can never look at each other the same way again. I hate what happened back there. I overpowered another man, fairly, and I had reason, but it wasn't enough. I wanted to humiliate him in front of his wife. I wanted him to feel small about himself in front of me. I could feel the bone in his arm about to snap like a dry, brittle wishbone. "Break the fucking arm." When he looked at me and said "Break the fucking arm" I didn't know who he was talking to. "Break the fucking arm." Jesus. Where was I? Whose arm was it? That could have been Chloe or one of the kids or one of them. In my head, I do it all the time. Cut ahead of me in traffic. Check your bank balance and start paying bills on the quick cash machine when there's a line. Say "Hunh?" with an accent when I ask you a question in perfectly good English. Fucking nigger, dumb cunt, idiot faggot. I kill a couple of hundred of them a day in my impotent fashion.

CHLOE. *(From within.)* John!

JOHN. In a minute! When I turned forty, my mother gave me a baby picture of myself. Everyone cooed and aahed but I took it as a reproach. There I am, golden curls, laughing, chipped front tooth, holding an apple. And now look at me. I've become a stranger

54

to the very woman who bore me. I just wish I knew the precise moment I stopped being that laughing child with apple and turned into this. I would go back there again and again until I understood it. I know the precise moment I almost broke my brother-in-law's arm.

CHLOE. *(From within.)* John!

JOHN. I'm on my way! Sally will never let me fuck her again. That pisses me off as much as it saddens me. We gave each other great pleasure. We can never talk about these things the way they really happened and what they really meant. There's no apology deep enough to undo what I did to Sam. None. I will say "I'm sorry" and he will accept my apology but they will just be words and lies to get us through the business of living.

SALLY. You could have really hurt him.

SAM. It isn't that bad.

JOHN. I'm sorry. Really, I...

SAM. Let's not ruin the girls' weekend because of us.

CHLOE. *(Standing at the door.)* Did you hear me?

SALLY. Maybe you should...

JOHN. Leave?

SAM. No.

CHLOE. Have you seen my lens case?

JOHN. You plugged it in in the kitchen, by the toaster.

CHLOE. I'd lose my head if I didn't have it screwed on tight!

> *We will see her enter the kitchen from inside the house and get her contact lenses. She comes outside and proceeds to put them in.*

JOHN. Maybe we should.

SAM. No, I said.

JOHN. If this is going to be awkward for everyone...!

SAM. It's not going to be awkward for me, you son of a bitch.

JOHN. We'll go. I'm sorry, Sally.

SAM. Why let my bad mood spoil everyone else's weekend? Three against one. The Good Mood-ers have it! The subject of premature departure is closed. Premature ejaculation I'm up for.

JOHN. *(To Sally.)* What do you think?

SALLY. No one's in a good mood, Sam. *(To John.)* Stay. Go. I don't care. Stay.

SAM. God, I'd like to jump into that pool!

SALLY. Why don't you?

SAM. We just ate. You have to wait an hour.

SALLY. You don't believe that!

SAM. I certainly do. Didn't your mother raise you that way? Ours did. Didn't she, sis?

CHLOE. Didn't who what?

SAM. Mom. Raise us to wait a full hour before going back in the water.

CHLOE. She certainly did. To the minute. There was a big clock at the municipal pool and if we had swallowed our last bit of hot dog and Coke at 12:39 we weren't allowed back in the water until the sweep hand hit 1:39 exactly. Not a moment sooner. Sam and I would be poised at the edge of the pool like Esther Williams and Johnny Weissmuller ready to dive back in the moment the hour was up.

SAM. I still can't.

CHLOE. It's a terrible legacy to carry around with you the rest of your life. I pray we haven't scarred Little John, Megan, and Benjamin like that. As soon as they eat, I throw them back into the pool. "Eat that wiener and swim, you kids!" I'm kidding, I'm kidding. Jesus! Who would throw children into a swimming pool?

SALLY. My father did. That's how I learned to swim. He threw David and me off the end of a pier.

CHLOE. What was he thinking?

SALLY. I don't think he was. All of a sudden we heard him saying "All children can swim, it's a natural instinct" and the next thing we knew he was picking us up and dropping us off the end. Plop, plop!

CHLOE. How old were you?

SALLY. Six or seven. David was two years younger.

CHLOE. Your father dropped a four-year-old child off the end of a pier?

SALLY. Maybe he was five. I don't remember exactly.

JOHN. What happened?

SALLY. I guess I instinctively knew what to do. I started paddling like a little dog but David went right to the bottom like a stone.

CHLOE. Did he drown? I mean, did he start to drown?

SALLY. He would have. Our father dove in and brought him up.

JOHN. That was big of him.

CHLOE. John hates his father.

JOHN. I do not.

CHLOE. Yes you do, darling. Don't interrupt.

SALLY. He just ignored David, like it had never happened and went back to drinking with his friends, but you could see he was disappointed in his son. Poor David. He looked so sad.

CHLOE. I wonder why. That's a terrible story. It sounds like your brother never had a chance.

SALLY. At what?

CHLOE. I know I'm not supposed to say "normal." "Straight" is the word I'm supposed to use. I hate it. It sounds like a ruler. And heterosexual is just plain ugh-y! I hate all those "O" words.

SALLY. I think the causes of our sexuality run a little deeper and are a hell of a lot more mysterious than being thrown off a pier.

CHLOE. It's entirely the parents' fault. If any of our three turned out that way, I would feel like killing myself. I probably wouldn't do it, actually, it is a mortal sin, after all, for those of us who still practice the faith of our fathers—

SAM. Don't start, Chloe!

CHLOE. —but I would feel like doing it. It's such a rejection! Can we change the subject? This is very depressing.

JOHN. You brought it up, Chloe.

CHLOE. I dredge everything up sooner or later. I'm a walking nerve end. I think these are very difficult times to be a parent in.

SALLY. I think these are very difficult times to be anything in.

JOHN. I'll drink to that.

SAM. This used to be a wonderful country.

JOHN. It still could be.

CHLOE. It still is. I mean, look at Russia.

SALLY. Now it's my turn: Can we change the subject?

CHLOE. Second!

JOHN. Is there a movie theatre anywhere on the island?

SAM. No! No bowling alley either. I don't know how people are supposed to entertain themselves.

CHLOE. I guess you've noticed, Sally, I've decided to let bygones be bygones. I don't believe in holding grudges.

SALLY. Neither do I. I'm sorry we keep getting off on the wrong foot.

CHLOE. Sally, may I make one teeny, teeny, teeny, teeny, tiny suggestion?

SALLY. Of course you may.

CHLOE. The next time you tell that story about your father and the swimming lesson, don't refer to yourself as paddling like a dog. It's a real put-down.

SALLY. Really? Thank you.

CHLOE. Thank *you. (Takes a deep breath.)* This ocean air is so calming! I'm sorry I took those pills. *(To Sam.)* Where are you going?

SAM. I feel a little sticky. I want to get this tea off me.

CHLOE. Why don't you just jump into the pool?

SAM. We've been through that.

SALLY. Be careful of the hot water. It's very hot. Scalding almost.

    Sam will use the outdoor shower during the following.

CHLOE. Does anyone mind if I practice out here?

JOHN. That depends on what you're going to practice.

CHLOE. *(To Sally.)* Ignore him. He's such a clown.

JOHN. We don't want any voodoo or black magic this weekend, Chloe. None of your witchcraft.

CHLOE. I left it all in Connecticut. This is strictly Mr. Frank Loesser, *Guys and Dolls: A Musical Fable of Broadway*, opening September 5 through October 10.*

> *Chloe goes inside.*

SAM. Ow!

SALLY. I warned you!

JOHN. *(To someone next door.)* Excuse me?

SAM. There's no soap!

SALLY. Yes, there is!

CHLOE. *(From within.)* Is there an outlet out there?

JOHN. *(To someone next door.)* Let me ask Mrs. Truman... Mrs. Truman, David's sister. *(To Sally.)* We've been asked next door to watch the fireworks tonight.

CHLOE. *(From within.)* Did you say something?

SALLY. I don't know. What do you think?

JOHN. I don't know.

SALLY. Can't we think about it?

JOHN. What is there to think about?

SALLY. Is it just going to be men?

JOHN. I didn't ask him. Hurry up. They're all looking over here.

> *Chloe comes out of her room with a portable cassette player.*

CHLOE. I don't need an outlet. I've got batteries. Dumb, dumb, dumb!

SALLY. *(To someone next door.)* Hello, I'm Sally Truman, David's—! ...You were there? ...It *was* beautiful... My brother-in-law told me. That's very kind of you. Unfortunately, we have other plans.

CHLOE. Who is she talking to?

JOHN. The neighbors.

CHLOE. What plans? What's happening?

---

* See Special Note on Songs/Recordings at the back of this volume.

SAM. Ow! Did someone flush the toilet?

SALLY. *(To someone next door.)* It sounds wonderful. I wish we'd known.

SAM. Who are you talking to? Who is she talking to?

CHLOE. Your neighbors.

SAM. What about?

CHLOE. What do I look like? Swami Lou, the Mind Reader?

SALLY. *(To someone next door.)* Not since the lawyer's. Have you been in touch with him? …Bridgehampton? That's out on Long Island? …Oh, I hope so. Well, nice shouting across a deck with you.

JOHN. *(To Chloe.)* See the guy in the yellow shirt?

CHLOE. Where?

JOHN. Don't just turn around and look. He'll see you.

SALLY. *(To someone next door.)* Oh, excuse me, but have you heard anything about a drowning?

CHLOE. Bright yellow?

JOHN. There's only one yellow.

SALLY. *(To someone next door.)* A drowning!

SAM. There's a big nest of something up there.

CHLOE. What about him?

SALLY. *(To someone next door.)* No, I don't *know* that there's been a drowning—

JOHN. I've seen him in our neck of the woods.

SAM. What is that? Hornets, wasps, what?

SALLY. *(To someone next door.)* I saw someone swim out and I didn't see him swim back!

CHLOE. Oooooooh.

JOHN. Oooooh? What does that mean, ooooooh?

CHLOE. He's cute.

SALLY. *(To someone next door.)* I'm sure you're right. I've always been a little frightened of the ocean.

CHLOE. *(To someone next door.)* With good reason! Her father threw her off a pier!

SAM. Ow!! Goddamnit, someone's flushing a toilet!

SALLY. No one's flushing a toilet. Chloe, please!

CHLOE. *(To someone next door.)* I hope you boys don't mind a little show.

JOHN. Leave them alone, Chloe.

SALLY. Don't call them boys, Chloe.

CHLOE. *(To someone next door.)* If you like what you see, send money. If you don't, I don't want to know. I have very thin skin.

SALLY. Chloe, they were only asking us over for drinks tonight. They weren't requesting a floor show.

CHLOE. Drinks? That's so nice of them! *(To someone next door.)* I'll bring some dip!

SAM. Will someone bring me a towel?

SALLY. I just got through telling them no.

JOHN. That word isn't in her vocabulary.

CHLOE. That's not true. *(To Sally.)* So we're not going over?

SAM. A towel, someone!

SALLY. I think it's best.

CHLOE. It's your house. *(To someone next door.)* I'll still send some dip over!

SAM. Would someone please bring me a towel?

John crosses to the bedroom to get a towel for Sam.

Thank you.

JOHN. How was it?

SAM. Great, except the water keeps getting red hot.

JOHN. Your neck is red. You've got a real line where your shirt was. I've got something that takes the sting out pretty good.

John hands Sam a towel.

SAM. Thank you.

JOHN. You've been losing weight.

SAM. Who? Me?

JOHN. God knows, I'm not. It's all that goddamn ice cream Chloe keeps bringing into the house.

CHLOE. *(To Sally.)* Look! The menfolk.

SALLY. I see them.

CHLOE. Knock on wood.

> *She knocks on her head. Sally goes into her room. Chloe sets up her portable cassette player. John is still talking to Sam, who is toweling off in the outdoor shower.*

JOHN. I guess you heard. They wanted us for drinks next door, the port side. We said no. Have you always had that mole there?

SAM. Would you mind...?

JOHN. I'm sorry.

SAM. I'm not real good at this locker-room stuff. I never was. If you'd just let me dry off and get some clothes on.

JOHN. I'm terribly sorry.

SAM. It's nothing personal.

JOHN. I don't take it as such.

SAM. Sally!

JOHN. She's in the house. What do you need?

SAM. A pair of shorts, *under*shorts! There's clean polo shirts in the drawer, I've got some blue slacks in the closet.

JOHN. Any particular color polo shirt?

SAM. It doesn't matter. Red, the red one.

JOHN. Anything else?

SAM. That's it, I think. Oh, a comb. In the bathroom.

JOHN. I'll be right back.

> *He goes into Sam and Sally's room. He gathers Sam's clothing. Chloe walks over to the shower.*

CHLOE. I'm so glad to see you two getting along or should I be waiting for the other shoe to drop?

SAM. Your husband turns on a dime. Prick, nice, prick, nice. I wish he'd make up his mind.

> *Chloe starts the cassette player. We hear clumsy piano playing.*

What the hell is that music?

CHLOE. It's Megan playing the chords to my number. I know it doesn't sound like much.

SAM. Jesus!

CHLOE. It's just chords for Christ's sake. Give the kid a break. Vladimir Horo-what's-his-hoosie couldn't do much with just chords.

SAM. What are you doing?

CHLOE. I want to see your dick.

SAM. What? No! Are you nuts?

CHLOE. Oh come on, I'm your big sister. Let me see it.

SAM. No.

CHLOE. I let you see my thing when I was in high school and you were still some little squirt in the fifth grade. You and your friend, Claude Barbizon, came into my bedroom. I didn't make *you* beg.

SAM. What drugs do you take? What cult have you joined?

CHLOE. When did you become such a prude?

SAM. I'm not a prude and I resent you saying that. I resent it very much.

CHLOE. It's not like I asked to see your bank balance.

SAM. I don't believe this.

CHLOE. Come on, let me see it. For old time's sake. I'll never ask you again. It's a one-time proposition.

SAM. There. Are you satisfied?

CHLOE. It's very nice.

SAM. Thank you.

CHLOE. I'm impressed.

SAM. Thank you.

CHLOE. And I'll tell you something. It's much bigger than you-know-who's, certainly in that state of flaccidity. Is that a word? I think I just made it up. You tell him I said that and I'll deny every word of it. My compliments to our parents.

We see John and Sally laughing and talking within the house.

SAM. What are they doing in there?

CHLOE. Talking.

63

SAM. I hear laughing.

CHLOE. All right, they're laughing.

SAM. Would you please see what your husband is doing with my wife?

CHLOE. Right now it looks like he's got her legs over her head in some Kama Sutra position we learned at Club Med.

Sam emerges from the shower with a towel around his waist and crosses to Chloe.

SAM. That's not funny.

CHLOE. I know.

SAM. Then you know?

CHLOE. I only know what I read in the paper.

SAM. He's fucking her.

CHLOE. He fucked her. It's over.

SAM. How do you know?

CHLOE. He told me.

SAM. And you believe him?

CHLOE. Yes.

SAM. Why?

CHLOE. I want to.

SAM. That's a wonderful reason.

CHLOE. You got a better one?

SAM. The truth.

CHLOE. That word has gotten more people into more trouble than all the lies that were ever told. Fuck the truth. It's more trouble than it's worth.

She goes back to her cassette and rewinds it to the beginning.

If I don't believe the son of a bitch, I've only got one option as I see it.

SAM. What's that?

CHLOE. Wait till he's sound asleep, take a hammer and bludgeon him to death.

Sam moves away and stubs his foot on the deck.

SAM. Ow!

CHLOE. What's the matter?

SAM. I got a splinter. Sally! Sally!

Sally comes out onto the deck, John following.

SALLY. What happened?

SAM. I got a splinter in my foot.

SALLY. Do we have a tweezers?

JOHN. I do.

He crosses deck to his and Chloe's room.

SALLY. Get off it! Let me see!

Sally helps Sam to sit.

SAM. I can't look! It's big! It's huge. It's in there about six inches.

SALLY. Let me look at it.

JOHN. *(From within.)* Honey, where's my Dopp kit?

CHLOE. I knew he was going to ask me that! *(To John.)* Try the bathroom. *(To Sally.)* I never know where anything is when we travel!

JOHN. *(From within.)* Got it!

CHLOE. Thank you!

She crosses herself.

SAM. Is there a hospital on the island?

SALLY. You're not going to need a hospital—!

John comes onto the deck.

I can't deal with this! It's a lulu.

SAM. What? What? It's a what? What's a lulu?

JOHN. Let me see.

SAM. I don't want you doing it—! I want Sally to!

Chloe has started her cassette going. She will begin to practice a song from a musical she is rehearsing. It will be a while before the others notice this going on while they deal with Sam's foot.

JOHN. Keep your foot still.

SAM. I am!

JOHN. Sally, hold his foot.

SAM. Do we have to make *The Song of Bernadette* out of this?

JOHN. Okay. Got it!

> *He yanks something out of Sam's foot.*

SAM. *(Erupting.)* Jesus Christ! You fucking bastard!

> *John holds up a sliver that is almost two inches long.*

JOHN. Look at that!

SALLY. Do you want to keep that down, Chloe?

CHLOE. Don't mind me! I'm just doing my thing. I can't deal with any kind of puncture of the human flesh.

JOHN. I'm going to sterilize a pin with a match and then I want to probe for any small slivers left in there.

SAM. The hell you are!

JOHN. It's the slivers that cause the infections.

SALLY. He's right.

SAM. Since when do you know so much about it?

JOHN. We need iodine.

SAM. No iodine.

SALLY. Try our medicine cabinet.

> *John goes into Sally and Sam's room.*

SAM. I don't want him rummaging around in the medicine cabinet.

SALLY. It's going to be fine.

SAM. I have put some extremely personal things in there. I don't want some stranger knowing certain things about me.

SALLY. He's just getting the iodine.

JOHN. *(From within.)* Got it!

SALLY. You're both impossible.

SAM. He's not probing around in my foot with a sterilized safety pin and that's that.

> *John returns with the iodine.*

JOHN. I found a pin on your dresser.

SAM. *(To Sally.)* You see? You see?

JOHN. Hold this.

> *He hands pin to Sally and lights a match.*

Do you want to knock that off, Petal?

CHLOE. I'll keep it low.

> *Indeed, we will barely be able to hear her as she mouths the words and does her steps.*

SAM. She's really very talented for a housewife. I actually preferred her Mame to Lucille Ball's.

> *John finishes sterilizing the pin.*

JOHN. Hold his foot again.

SAM. I want Sally to do that.

JOHN. Okay.

> *He hands pin to Sally and steps aside.*

SALLY. Now don't move. I don't want to hurt you.

SAM. I'll be brave, mama.

> *She works on his foot. Chloe is still singing sotto voce and dancing to the clumsy piano accompaniment playing on the cassette. John moves apart from the others. He looks at Chloe practicing her number.*

JOHN. You're looking good, Petal!

CHLOE. Give me five more weeks! Can we call the kids tonight? I gave Mima the number here but you know how cheap she is.

JOHN. I'll tell Mother you said so. Yes, we'll call! Hey! I love you.

CHLOE. What?

JOHN. You heard me.

> *He goes to the edge of the deck and looks out to the ocean.*

SALLY. When did your feet get so callused and bunioned and corny?

SAM. Those aren't bunions. Old people have bunions. Stick to the splinter. Ow!

SALLY. I'm sorry.

SAM. Ow!

SALLY. I said I was sorry!

SAM. That's enough.

Sam takes the pin away from Sally and begins to work on his own foot. The lights are coming down on Chloe silently singing and dancing, John watching her, and Sam bent over his foot. Sally stands and looks out to sea. Very strong special on Sally. Her eyes tell us that she has seen something on the shore.

SALLY. Oh my God. Drowned.

The light snaps off.

End of Act Two

ACT THREE

Night. There is a full moon and many, many stars. The main source of light is the pool. There is an ultraviolet bug lamp, which we will hear zapping insects throughout the act.

There are two noisy parties going on in the two next-door houses. A lively up-tempo rendition of a classic from the American Song Book is coming from one house while a very contemporary rock group is heard from the other. The two sounds should not complement each other.

The wind has stopped blowing. It is warm and muggy, a perfect night for a midnight dip.

Sam is playing with the telescope, Sally is washing dishes in the kitchen, John is on a cordless telephone, Chloe is in her room, dressing.

SAM. This is fabulous! The clarity! You can see everything! John, have you—?

JOHN. *(On the phone.)* I don't think you want to do that, son.

SAM. *(Calling off.)* Sally! Come out here!

JOHN. *(On the phone.)* What does your grandmother say? *(Calling off.)* Chloe! *(On the phone.)* Well where is she? *(Calling off.)* Chloe! Goddamnit!

> *Sam goes to the sliding screen door and speaks to Sally, who is still working in the kitchen.*

SAM. Honey, come on, you gotta see this. It's like being in a planetarium. You've never seen so many stars. It will get your mind off what happened this afternoon.

JOHN. *(Covering phone, to Sam.)* They want to go on a hayride in the rain. Their grandmother is at her Weight Watchers meeting. Count your blessings.

> *John sees limp kite string.*

My kite's down. Shit! When did this happen?

SAM. *(To John.)* You really ought to take a look through this.

JOHN. When did my kite come down?

SAM. I assume it was when the wind stopped. *(Under his breath.)* You don't have to be Isaac Newton to figure that one out.

JOHN. I was trying to break a record.

CHLOE. *(From within.)* Did somebody say something?

JOHN. *(On the phone.)* Have Mima call us the minute she gets back. Your uncle Sam wants to talk to you. He's pulling the phone out of my hand. Stop it, Sam! I don't think your uncle Sam thinks it's a good idea to go hayriding in the rain either. *(Hands phone to Sam.)* Tell them they can't go hayriding in the goddamn rain for Christ's sake, will you?

SAM. *(Into phone.)* Hello?

John goes to door of his room and speaks to Chloe.

JOHN. They want to go for a hayride in a rainstorm! Mrs. Dietrich says it's all right. My mother's at a goddamn Weight Watchers meeting! She's at the wrong meeting! She should be at AA. Why didn't somebody tell me my kite had come down?

He will start reeling in the string.

SAM. *(On the phone.)* I'm sorry Megan, I thought you were Little John. *(To John.)* Which one did you give me?

JOHN. I don't know. They're all on there. Different extensions. *(To Sally, within.)* They want to go for a hayride in a rainstorm. *(To Sam.)* Tell them they could be electrocuted!

SAM. You could get electrocuted!

JOHN. You know, struck by lightning! *(To Sally, within.)* I was just telling Sam: Count your blessings.

CHLOE. *(From within.)* John, did you see my—? Never mind, I've got it!

Sally comes out onto the deck drying a large pasta pot.

SAM. *(Into phone.)* All right, everybody shut up! Listen, kids, your aunt Sally is dying to talk to you. She's grabbing the phone from me.

He hands phone to Sally.

They want to go for a hayride in the rain. Maybe they'll listen to their aunt. Chloe!

He crosses to screen door outside Chloe's room.

SALLY. *(Into phone.)* Hello? Children? This is your aunt Sally. Now just a minute—!

SAM. *(To Chloe.)* They want to go for a hayride in a lightning storm!

CHLOE. *(From within.)* Do you think this top matches this bottom?

SAM. What do I know? You're the clotheshorse.

CHLOE. *(From within.)* Sammy!

SAM. You're asking the wrong person. I think you always look great. Is that the new *Life* magazine? Can I take a—?

SALLY. *(Into phone.)* All right, now it's my turn. The reason your father doesn't want you to go for a hayride in the rain is that he loves you and he doesn't want anything to happen to you while he's away and unable to protect you. You could catch a cold. You could be struck by lightning. What else could happen to you if you go for a hayride in the rain? That should be enough, Benjamin.

JOHN. It won't be.

SALLY. *(To John.)* Who is Mrs. Dietrich?

JOHN. A neighbor.

SALLY. That's what parents do: love their children and protect them from the dangers of the world. If I had children, they would be so safe. They would never be alone. I would never let them go.

John puts his hand on her arm.

Don't touch me.

JOHN. I'm sorry.

SALLY. *(Into phone.)* I'm feeling very sad and angry and unlistened to right now. That's why it's so important you understand me. I saw a terrible thing this afternoon. I saw what happens when we're not loved and protected and we feel so alone.

JOHN. You're not alone, Sally.

SALLY. *(Into phone.)* I saw a man who drowned in the ocean.

JOHN. Jesus, Sally, don't—

SALLY. *(Into phone.)* He was very young. Even though his features were swollen from the water, he was very handsome. Nobody wanted to look at him like this, but I made myself.

JOHN. We all told you not to go down there.

SALLY. *(Into phone.)* I wanted to see what death looks like and not be afraid of it.

JOHN. What kind of thing is that to say to a child?

SALLY. *(Into phone.)* Oh, he could swim all right, Megan. He could swim too well too far. I saw him swim out this morning. I knew he wouldn't come back and I didn't do anything.

JOHN. Jesus, Sally, you're scaring them.

John takes the phone from her.

SALLY. Our eyes had met.

JOHN. Children, this is your father again.

SALLY. His wave did acknowledge me.

JOHN. Now settle down.

SALLY. I let him swim out never to return.

JOHN. Aunt Sally's still upset by what happened. We all are.

He continues but we don't hear him.

SALLY. My eyes didn't say "Stay, life is worth living." They said "Go, God speed, God bless." My wave didn't say "Hurry back, young man, happiness awaits you ashore." It said "Goodbye, I know where you're going. I've wanted to go there too." I knew his secret, and he knew mine. Even from a great distance we know so much about each other but spend our lives pretending we don't. He wanted to die and I helped him. Oh children, children, such perils await you, such pain and no one to protect us.

She touches her stomach.

Don't you leave me. Stick around this time.

JOHN. Aunt Sally's still upset by what happened. We all are.

Chloe opens the screen door with a flourish. She has changed into a snappy resort-wear ensemble.

CHLOE. Ta-da! How do I look?

JOHN. *(Into phone.)* Your mother wants to talk to you. She's tearing the phone out of my hand.

CHLOE. Don't tell them that. They're spoiled enough. Do I match?

JOHN. *(Holding phone to Chloe.)* They want to go on a hayride in the rain.

CHLOE. You mean that hasn't been settled yet? I swear, sometimes I don't know what fathers are for. The mothers do everything.

She takes phone from John and speaks into it.

Hello, this is Mommy. No. N–o. *Nada. Rien.* Forget the hayride. The hayride is out. Got that? *(To Sally.)* You just have to be firm with them. Don't be intimidated by them, like they were something special. They're just little people. That's all you have to remember about them.

JOHN. *(To Sally.)* Does Sam know you get like this?

CHLOE. *(Into phone.)* Is that all settled now? Is everything under control?

JOHN. Does he?

SALLY. I hope not.

JOHN. I mean…why? What's wrong?

SALLY. I don't know.

CHLOE. *(Into phone.)* The next time you go to Mima's we'll be sure there's a Nintendo there. We'll give her one for Christmas.

JOHN. *(To Sally.)* Your brother?

SALLY. I don't know.

JOHN. Is it you and Sam?

SALLY. No.

JOHN. Was it us?

SALLY. I said I don't know.

She moves away from him.

Sam, what are you doing in there?

SAM. *(From within.)* There's an incredible article in here on jellyfish.

JOHN. Why won't you talk to me?

SALLY. There's nothing to say.

SAM. *(From within.)* You can die from them! The pictures are disgusting.

CHLOE. *(Into phone.)* I'm sure Aunt Sally didn't mean to frighten you.

JOHN. Please, Sally, don't be like this.

SAM. *(From within.)* Look at this guy's face from them.

SALLY. I don't know how else to be.

SAM. *(From within.)* His chest, his arms!

JOHN. It's not fair.

SALLY. I'm sorry.

CHLOE. *(Into phone.)* She was upset. We all were. It was a terrible thing. You should see me, I'm a wreck. I hope you children never, ever see anything so dreadful.

> *Sam comes back onto the deck with a copy of* Life *magazine.*

SAM. You want to see something to turn your stomach? And this is supposed to be a family magazine!

> *He will show a picture in the magazine to John.*

Imagine if those things got wrapped around your dick.

JOHN. I'd rather not.

SAM. *(To Sally.)* Honey, take a look at this. They're called Portuguese man o' wars. I'd rather swim in this pool than risk my tender gonads to one of those suckers. And all you were worried about was sharks!

CHLOE. *(Into phone.)* Aunt Sally's sorry if she upset you.

SALLY. That's not true, Chloe.

CHLOE. *(Holding phone to Sally.)* Tell them you're sorry, Sally.

SALLY. But I'm not.

CHLOE. It doesn't matter. Tell them anyway.

SALLY. Why?

CHLOE. For me.

SALLY. What about for me?

CHLOE. They're children. It's not fair.

JOHN. Leave Sally alone, Chloe.

SAM. What did she do?

CHLOE. Upset my children. *(Into phone.)* Hold on.

SAM. Your children are always upset. What did you say, honey?

SALLY. I told them to be careful. To be very, very careful.

SAM. What's wrong with that?

CHLOE. You told them you'd seen the face of death and that there was no one to protect them.

SALLY. Not them, us. All of us.

CHLOE. Be that as it may—!

SALLY. There isn't, Chloe.

SAM. What are you talking about?

JOHN. I've tried. Maybe she'll tell you.

CHLOE. Well it scared them!

SALLY. Good. I want to scare everyone tonight.

JOHN. She told them how alone she was.

SAM. Alone? With all of us here? Honey, that's nuts!

CHLOE. Please! Tell them something comforting.

SALLY. I don't know how to talk to children. I don't know what they want to hear.

CHLOE. The same thing we all do. That they're loved. That they're safe.

SALLY. But we're not.

CHLOE. That's your opinion.

SALLY. Then you tell them, Chloe.

CHLOE. They have to hear it from you.

SALLY. I'm sorry, I can't.

> She sits at the edge of the pool and dangles her feet in the
> water.

Has anyone been in the pool yet?

CHLOE. *(Into phone.)* Aunt Sally is very sorry if she said anything to upset you. She doesn't have children of her own so she says things she doesn't mean. Your father wants to talk to you.

JOHN. I've already spoken to them—

CHLOE. He's grabbing the phone from me.

She gives the phone to John and heads for her room.

That really wasn't very nice of you, Sally.

SALLY. I'm tired of being nice.

Sam sits by her side at the edge of the pool. Chloe will change into another outfit.

JOHN. *(Into phone.)* Mom, thank God you're back. We can't deal with this hayride thing long distance. Will you talk some sense into them—?

SAM. What's the matter, honey? Tell me.

JOHN. *(Into phone.)* Thank you. What magic sway do grandparents have over children their real parents don't? Oh, something they thought their aunt said they completely misunderstood. Wait a minute, I'm losing you!

He fusses with the antenna on the cordless phone and wanders to another part of the deck that is out of sight to us.

SAM. You don't want to talk about it?

Sally shakes her head.

JOHN. *(Off.)* So how was Weight Watchers? It's a racket, like everything else. How much have you lost? That's great. We're going to have to get you a bikini for Mother's Day. Wonderful weekend. Beautiful house. Clear as a bell. There's a full moon, stars. We could use a little breeze. It's very still. Muggy almost. Everything is soggy. The sheets, the towels. Hello? There you go again. Hello?

SAM. Okay.

They both sit, dangling their feet in the pool. The sound of the bug lamp is very "heard." The party sounds have pretty much become second-nature to us now, i.e., we are scarcely aware of them, unless there is a particularly loud outburst of laughter.

Look, I think we all feel terrible about what happened this afternoon. It's put a damper on everything. I don't know how those guys can act like nothing happened. Was he a friend of David's? Did you find out?

SALLY. Nobody seemed to know who he was.

SAM. He must have come from somewhere.

SALLY. They checked every house.

John reappears with the cordless phone in his hand.

JOHN. They haven't perfected these things yet. Not that we were talking about anything important. Where's Chloe?

SAM. Inside.

JOHN. Am I interrupting anything?

SAM. I wish you were.

JOHN. Mind if I join you? Chloe!

He sits on the edge of the pool and dangles his feet in the water.

That feels good!

SAM. Why don't you go in?

JOHN. Maybe later. Why don't you and Sally?

SAM. I still feel that steak and baked potato and corn on the cob and strawberry shortcake with real whipped cream right here. I'd sink like a rock.

SALLY. None of us are ever going to go into that pool so can we just stop talking about it?

CHLOE. *(From within.)* Did somebody say something?

SALLY. We all think it's infected. We all think it's polluted. We all think we'll get AIDS and die if we go in.

JOHN. That's not quite true, Sally.

SALLY. One drop of water in your mouth or on an open sore and we'll be infected with my brother and his black lover and God knows who else was in here. Pissing, ejaculating. I think we're very brave to dangle our feet like this. They may fall off.

CHLOE. *(From within.)* If you have something to say to me, John, come in here and say it. I cannot hear through walls or screens or whatever they are! Partitions!

JOHN. When did you develop this uncanny ability of yours to say absolutely the most inappropriate thing you could think of?

SALLY. Everybody's thinking them. I've merely decided to say them.

> *She splashes John.*

JOHN. Stop that!

SALLY. Close your mouth!

JOHN. Sally, stop it, I said!

SAM. Sally!

SALLY. You afraid of the water?

> *She splashes him, too.*

Everybody's afraid of dying around here!

JOHN. If you can't control your wife, Sam!

SALLY. I can't believe I heard that. Have some more water, Mr. Haddock!

SAM. Sally!!

SALLY. Come on, Sam, you heard the man. Control me! Your wife is out of control. Do something!

> *She splashes Sam.*

It's your last chance to be a man!

> *She stops splashing him and scoops up water from the pool in the palm of her hand and drinks it.*

Then let's all get AIDS and die!

> *Sam knocks her hand away from her mouth. He grabs and holds her right wrist. She pulls him to her with her other hand and kisses him very hard and long on the mouth.*

I love you.

SAM. Jesus, Sally, what's gotten into you?

SALLY. Thank you for not being a man. Thank you for not controlling your wife.

> *She kisses him again. He pulls away from her and tries to clear his mouth. Clearly, he is not comfortable with the thought of the taste of her mouth in his. He gets up from the edge of the pool.*

SAM. Stop that! I don't want to kiss you. I'm sorry your brother died but it's not my fault. I didn't kill him. I don't know about pools and AIDS and homosexuals. I don't want to. It frightens me, all right? All of this! I'm sorry, I can't help it, it's who I am. Excuse me.

He goes quickly into their room and exits into the bathroom beyond.

JOHN. That was ugly, Sally.

SALLY. That's your opinion.

JOHN. Ugly to watch, ugly to listen to.

SALLY. I don't think so. I don't want to be married to a man who thinks he can control his wife. Or wants to. Or needs to. Or thinks he has a right to. I would hate being married to you. Sam doesn't do anything. That's why I married him.

Sam is heard gargling Listerine off.

JOHN. That's charming.

SALLY. I needed you very badly that weekend.

JOHN. So did I. I won't pretend I wasn't hoping it would happen again.

SALLY. I'm sorry. You may not believe this but you are almost the only other man I've been with but Sam.

JOHN. I figured as much.

SALLY. How come?

JOHN. Something about you. Passionate but not promiscuous. Maybe you could help me. Was it my breath?

SALLY. Your breath was very sweet. I wanted the parts you don't give to anyone else. Your secrets, your fears. Not the parts of you that connect us, the parts that separate.

JOHN. No one gets them, Sally.

SALLY. Not even Chloe?

JOHN. Especially Chloe.

SALLY. Don't you want everything from another person?

JOHN. No. I respect the distance between people. I rather like it, in fact.

SALLY. Why?

79

JOHN. To know me is not necessarily to like me. I'm afraid to run that risk.

SALLY. Right now I feel much closer to you than I ever did when we were making love. You're not even pretending to let me in.

JOHN. What you want from a man, you can never have.

SALLY. That will never stop me wanting it.

JOHN. Look, there's a ring down there.

SALLY. It's my brother's.

JOHN. Would you like me to get it for you?

SALLY. You're not afraid of the pool?

JOHN. Not everyone is dying from AIDS, Sally. There are other malevolent forces at work on God's miraculous planet.

SALLY. What's that supposed to mean?

Chloe comes back onto the deck. She is wearing a different outfit.

CHLOE. I don't care what anybody says: I didn't match! This matches. Where's Sam? I've decided not to let you get my goat, Sally.

SALLY. That's a very good decision, Chloe.

John has started retrieving the ring.

CHLOE. John, are you sure you want to do that?

JOHN. I'm sure.

He splashes some pool water on her.

CHLOE. Stop that! Are you insane?

JOHN. Sally thinks we're all afraid of getting AIDS! Are we, Chloe? Come on, let's show her we're not.

CHLOE. That's very, very, very funny. Sam!

JOHN. She's figured out why no one is using her brother's beautiful pool.

CHLOE. Including her, I noticed.

JOHN. Sally's not afraid. She drank the water. She scooped it up and drank it. I think Sally was right. I think we should all get AIDS and die.

CHLOE. What are you doing?

JOHN. I don't know, Chloe.

He plunges his head into the pool and blows out his breath there, making the water bubble.

CHLOE. Stop that! John! I said stop! This is all your fault. You've been morbid and disruptive ever since we got here. Sam! Sam!!

Sam comes out on the deck.

You're frightening me, John!

SAM. What's he doing?

CHLOE. Make him stop it, Sam.

SALLY. That's enough, John.

SAM. Come on, John, enough's enough.

No one moves. They all watch John. John stops moving. He stops blowing out air. His head and shoulders float motionless on the water's surface. There is an enormous burst of laughter from one of the parties on either side. Sam grabs John by the shoulders and lifts his head out of the pool and lets his body roll heavily on his back on the deck. John looks like he's dead. Sam turns away from him. Chloe bends over his body. John spurts a stream of pool water in her face. Chloe doesn't flinch.

JOHN. Now we're all infected.

CHLOE. Just so long as you're all right. You're my life.

John takes one of her hands and begins to kiss the fingers.

I should take my hand away. I don't want to.

JOHN. Thank God for these dear, familiar fingers.

CHLOE. My hand is paralyzed. He needs it so much right now, to heal his shame.

SALLY. When I was at the hospital with David and he'd lost his sight, he would put his fingers on my face "to remember me," as he put it. "To remember me."

SAM. I am watching two men make love in the bushes next to the house. It's probably poison ivy but they don't care. They are in the throes of passion.

JOHN. Fingers that have stroked and held me. Prepared our food. Diapered our children.

CHLOE. It would be like taking a teat away from a child. Even if I wanted to, I couldn't. I want him to need me like this.

SALLY. He would touch my eyes, my mouth. His hands would trace my profile over and over.

SAM. Is that what we look like when we make love? I see huffing and puffing and biting and licking and kissing and hugging and grunting and groaning but I don't hear anyone say "I love you."

JOHN. See! The first faint tracings of a liver spot. She will grow old without me.

CHLOE. I'm as close to love as he's ever going to get and that suffices. It shouldn't but it does.

SALLY. I hated his fingers on my face. I hated the smells in his room. I hated him being gay. And yet I loved him. Who he'd been. Not what he'd become.

SAM. Now one man throws his head back, utters a cry, his body shudders and he lies still. Now the other: head jerking back, oh!, shudder, shudder, shudder, still.

JOHN. Familiar, pedestrian, banal fingers of a woman who was foolish enough to want to share her life with me. I feel such guilt before such uncomplicated goodness.

CHLOE. You are my life. I don't know what I'm going to do.

SALLY. I thought he was my best friend. And then there was Aaron. No warning, no indication. Just a matter-of-fact "Sis, this is Aaron." You don't put people out of your heart so quickly, not if you love them.

SAM. They still don't move. They lie in each other's arms on the sand, in the poison ivy, under a full July moon, the sound of the Atlantic Ocean and Ella Fitzgerald wondering "How High the Moon." And now I hear it. I hear "I love you."

There is a burst of color in the night sky above them. The Fourth of July fireworks have begun. Each new display will be greeted with a chorus of "ooh"s and "aah"s from the houses on either side of theirs.

CHLOE. Look! Fireworks! A full moon! The ocean! The Fourth of July! Sally, if you don't keep this house you should have your head examined. *(To John.)* Darling, why don't you go inside and change? You'll catch cold.

JOHN. I'm fine. Look at that, will you?

CHLOE. At least let me get you a towel.

> *She will go into their room and bring out a towel and dry John's hair for him.*

SALLY. This is like that scene in that movie with Cary Grant and Ava Gardner.

SAM. Here we go again! What movie, Sally?

SALLY. *Catching a Thief.*

SAM. Thank God for small arms control!

JOHN. Leave her alone, Sam.

SAM. People like you don't deserve the movies.

> *Chloe comes out of her room with a towel and begins to dry John's hair as he sits and watches the fireworks.*

JOHN. Ow!

CHLOE. What's wrong?

JOHN. You're toweling too hard.

CHLOE. You want me to get you a dry shirt?

JOHN. I'm fine.

SAM. There we go! That's the best one yet. *(Calling next door.)* Aren't these fabulous? Makes you proud to be an American. I hope you had your hot dogs and hamburgers and apple pie for today!

JOHN. *(Calling off.)* Excuse me? Are you talking to—? Thank you. The same to you. Do we have any what? *(To others on deck.)* Do we have any flags to wave?

SAM. What are you getting us into?

JOHN. *(Calling off.)* We left all our flags in Connecticut! That's all right, you don't have to do that—! The fireworks will be over before you know it—!

> *A packet of small American flags held together with a rubber*

band is tossed onto the deck. John catches them and will distribute them.

(Calling off.) Thank you.

Red, white, and blue streamers and confetti are being tossed down onto the deck from the taller houses on each side.

SAM. *(Calling off.)* Thank you. Thank you. *(To others on deck.)* They gonna come over here tomorrow and clean this mess up?

CHLOE. Don't be so ungracious. It's the Fourth of July.

SAM. I know. Just don't make it sound like Christmas Eve and we're the Cratchits.

The fireworks are reaching a noisy, colorful climax. Lots of different colors are exploding in the sky. The noise is deafening at the very end of this final barrage. John has given everyone a small American flag to wave.

CHLOE. Happy Fourth everyone! *Vive les États-Unis* and the republic for which it stands!

SAM. What are we supposed to do?

JOHN. Just wave your flag.

SAM. I feel like an idiot.

They are watching the fireworks explode above them and waving their flags.

CHLOE. John, remind me to remind Little Theatre we haven't done *The Music Man* in ages.

She starts to sing "America the Beautiful." John and Sam join in lustily. Sally sings, too, but more quietly. She is crying. Halfway through their singing their voices will be drowned out by the barrage of fireworks. In the first silence after the fireworks, the bug lamp will seem very loud again.

JOHN. I guess that's it.

SAM. There's usually one last—.

There is a final, thunderous report.

There it is. *(Calling off.)* Happy Fourth to you too. Thank you.

CHLOE. *À bientôt! À demain! Ciao! (To others.)* Quick, quick, quick! How do you say it in Jewish—? *(She's got it.) Shalom! Bonsoir!*

84

Guttenacht! (To others on the deck.) There's something about the ocean. I feel so fucking liberated by it. Now who wants what? Sally, a white wine spritzer, *n'est-ce pas?*

She will start making a round of drinks for everyone.

SALLY. That's all right.

CHLOE. The night is young, the stars are clear. I'm making you a spritzer. I know what you two lushes want. I'm having a Diet Pepsi. I have to be thin, thin, thin for Miss Adelaide. That costume designer has me practically naked.

Sam comes up to Sally, who has moved away since the singing and who is still quietly crying. At the same time, John goes into his and Chloe's room and draws the drapes. Perhaps we can see his silhouette against them.

SAM. Are you all right?

SALLY. *(Nodding.)* I'm fine. It's a stirring song.

CHLOE. *(Calling over to them.)* Chablis or Soave, Sally—? Oh, you two are talking! *Fermez la bouche,* Chloe. John? Now where's he gone to?

SALLY. I didn't think I'd feel David so strongly this weekend. Sometimes I feel I can't breathe.

SAM. We don't have to decide about the house tonight.

SALLY. What did we tell that lawyer?

SAM. That we'd be in touch. That's all. That we'd be in touch. You know, we could keep it and rent it.

SALLY. Look, they're dancing up there. Both houses.

SAM. That's not all some of them are doing.

SALLY. I wish I had a better opinion about all this.

SAM. I know. It's hard.

SALLY. Seeing them touching sort of sickens me. I can't help it. I was glad I never saw my brother dancing with another man and now I never will.

She breaks down and cries. Sam comforts her.

SAM. I'm right here.

SALLY. And yet if we had a child and they grew up that way, I know I would love them all the same. I know I would, I know it. But my love stops right there. It can't go any further.

SAM. It's okay, nobody's judging you.

SALLY. I'm judging myself.

SAM. If we had a child, he wouldn't grow up that way. I know it, I just know it. We would do everything right, so he wouldn't, and then even if he did, or her, you're right, we would love them all the same. But it won't happen. I'd be willing to bet my life on it.

CHLOE. Soup's on! Come and get it!

SAM. Come on, a little drink will do you good. *(Calling to Chloe.)* I'll get John.

SALLY. There's something I want to tell you before the weekend is over.

SAM. Okay. There's something I want to tell you. *(To Chloe.)* I'll raise His Highness!

> *He pulls back the drape of John's room.*

John?

> *He goes into their room.*

SALLY. Do you need any help?

CHLOE. Why thank you, Sally! Where's Sam?

SALLY. He's in with John.

> *Sam comes out of John's room.*

SAM. *(Over his shoulder, to John.)* I'm sorry.

SALLY. What's wrong?

SAM. I'm not sure.

> *Chloe comes forward with a tray of drinks.*

CHLOE. *Voilà les caps du nuit!* Nightcaps! John, don't hibernate in there. We're going to finish trouncing these two in charades.

SAM. He'll be right out. Sis, what's up. I've never seen so many pills as he's got in there. I didn't knock, I'm sorry. From the look on his face, you'd think I caught him shooting up.

CHLOE. John was diagnosed with cancer of the esophagus six weeks ago. We don't talk about it. We're going to fight it. They don't think they can operate. The pills are aggressive therapy. Don't ask me what that means. We're going to fight and hope. Hope and fight.

SALLY. Chloe, I'm so sorry.

CHLOE. You're not supposed to know. Either of you. He'll kill me.

SAM. You're my sister.

CHLOE. John sees the world as everyone else and him. We're all against him. A director said to me last month, "Why I believe those are real tears you're crying, Mrs. Haddock! Where did they come from? It's only *Oklahoma!*" "I guess I'm one of those Method actresses you read about, Jan," I told him. "Just one of those Method actresses."

>*She begins to cry. Sam takes the tray from her. Sally puts her arms around her. John comes out of the bedroom.*

There he is. There's my man. Now I'm holding you all to your promise. Sally, you go first. It was your turn. You were in last place.

SALLY. We don't have to play anymore —!

CHLOE. I insist. I've been looking forward to it all evening.

SAM. I'm sorry, John, I should have knocked.

JOHN. She hadn't told you?

SAM. Not a word. If there's anything I can—?

JOHN. There is, actually. You can die for me.

SAM. That's not funny.

JOHN. Well then don't ask, my friend.

CHLOE. Come on, Sally, choose a title or a phrase or a—.

SAM. Not a title, for God's sake, don't encourage her.

JOHN. What's happening?

CHLOE. Sshh! No talking. We're beginning. It's Sally's turn. I'm timing her. Ready, set, go! Well go, Sally, don't just stand there. The clock is running.

>*Sally is not very good at playing charades. It's an ordeal for her, from beginning to end, but she's trying to be a good sport. Each word costs her a great effort and is very painful.*

What are you doing?

SALLY. I don't know.

CHLOE. Have you chosen your category?

SALLY. No.

CHLOE. Sally!

SALLY. I have to choose a category?

CHLOE. You know you do. What were you doing all afternoon? I'm stopping the clock. Now choose a category.

SAM. Honey, if you don't want to play charades—

SALLY. I've got one.

CHLOE. You're sure? It's something we've all heard of? I hate *recherché* charades. I'm starting the clock.

Sally acts out her category.

A book? A play? A movie?

JOHN. A famous disease?

SAM. A song title?

SALLY. Yes!

CHLOE. No, dear, you can't talk, remember? Put your finger on your nose when we guess it. Now how many words in your song title?

Sally counts on her fingers.

They say it's going to be nice tomorrow.

SAM. This is torture for her.

CHLOE. Torture for her?

JOHN. I love avoidance!

CHLOE. You invented it.

SALLY. I think "eight."

SAM. What do you mean, you "think" eight? Just count them.

SALLY. Some are, you know, squished together—I don't know if they're one word or two.

SAM. Just make a choice!

SALLY. All right, seven!

SAM. Seven now!

CHLOE. She's not supposed to be talking. I'm sorry but I think there should be a penalty for that.

JOHN. I do, too. One multiple sclerosis for Sally.

CHLOE. Ignore him. First word.

SALLY. I can't do the first word.

CHLOE. Then do the second word.

Sally shakes her head.

Why not?

SALLY. I'm doing the second word. It's "no."

SAM. Do the third word, honey.

SALLY. I can't. It's too hard.

SAM. Then do the fourth. *(To Chloe.)* I could kill you right now.

CHLOE. All right, we'll play teams. Help her. But hurry up, I'm not stopping the clock.

Sam goes to Sally. She whispers in his ear.

Can I get you anything?

JOHN. They know.

CHLOE. I had to tell someone. He's my brother. She's his wife.

SAM. *(To Sally.)* What? Say it again?

SALLY. "There's no business like—"

SAM. Not out loud! That's it! We give up! Forfeit! Let's have another drink! John? Another drink?

CHLOE. What was it, Sally, your song title?

SALLY. "There's no business like the show business."

SAM. There's no "the" in it. It's "There's No Business Like Show Business" period.

CHLOE. That doesn't sound right.

SAM. Of course it doesn't sound right. It's wrong.

CHLOE. No, "There's No Business Like Show Business." There's a word missing. Sally's right, there is a "the" there. "There's No Business Like The Show Business."

JOHN. "There's No Business Like The Show Business." It doesn't make sense without the "the." You don't say "auto industry." You say "the" Auto Industry, "the" garment industry.

SALLY. I thought I was right.

SAM. I'm losing my mind! Sing it! "There's no business—"

CHLOE. "—like the show business."

SAM. *(Calling to the next house.)* Let's go to the experts! Excuse me! Yoo-hoo! Fellas!

SALLY. He hates to be wrong.

JOHN. You owe your wife an apology, Sam.

SAM. *(Turning away from the next house.)* They don't hear me. They're all doing the twist or something.

CHLOE. I doubt if they're doing the twist. Does that date you! The twist, Sally!

JOHN. We all agree. You're wrong. Just say it.

SAM. "There's no business like the show business."

CHLOE. Well, if you say it like that—mockingly.

SAM. "There's no business like the show business."

JOHN. Right!

SAM. "There's No Business Like Show Business."

CHLOE. Wrong!

SAM. Yeah? I could have sworn…! Are you sure? "There's No Business Like The Show Business." It sounds right now.

JOHN. It *is* right. Talk about stubborn!

SALLY. That's why he grinds his teeth in his sleep. He sets himself against the tide and won't go with it.

CHLOE. When did you start grinding your teeth in your sleep?

SAM. I don't know that I do. This is her opinion.

CHLOE. John grinds his teeth in his sleep.

JOHN. I do not.

CHLOE. I think all men grind their teeth in their sleep. It's their brutal nature expressing itself.

SALLY. If he keeps it up, Dr. Roston says he's not going to have any teeth left. They're getting all worn down. Show her.

SAM. No!

CHLOE. Let me see. Sam! I'm your sister.

She takes his face in her hands. Sam opens his mouth while Chloe looks in. John looks over her shoulder to see, too.

Oh my God, you're right. I see what you mean. Like stubs, some of them are. Hold still! What's that?

SALLY. *(Looks into Sam's mouth.)* I don't know what that is. I never saw that before. Sam, when did you get that?

JOHN. It looks like an abscess.

Sam succeeds in pulling away from Chloe.

SAM. Why don't you charge admission and sell tickets? I don't have an abscess. Fuck you!

CHLOE. Keep grinding and you're not going to have any teeth left. You either, Mr. Haddock.

JOHN. I don't grind my teeth.

SAM. Neither do I. I clench my jaws sometimes maybe but I don't get down there and grind.

SALLY. It's a horrible sound. I can't sleep. Tell John how Dr. Roston is treating you.

SAM. No. It's stupid.

SALLY. He wants him to fall asleep saying "Lips together, teeth apart" over and over again to himself.

JOHN. "Lips together, teeth apart"?

SAM. It's very romantic. "What did you say, darling?" "Nothing, dearest, lips together, teeth apart. Do you want to make love tonight? Lips together, teeth apart."

CHLOE. Does it work?

SAM. I don't grind my teeth.

SALLY. He won't even try it. I'm the one who falls asleep saying it for him. "Lips together, teeth apart."

JOHN. I believe you do. That sounds very loving. I'm jealous.

CHLOE. Do you want to fall asleep with me saying that? "Lips together, teeth apart"? I'll do it, lover. I guess this means it's the end of charades?

SALLY. Please, Chloe. We're all dreadful at them.

SAM. Speak for yourself.

JOHN. Look, I don't want my health to be an issue this weekend or any other. With or without cancer I'm still the same person, so there's no reason to change your opinion of me. I mean, riddled with the stuff, I'm still going to be the same rotten son of a bitch. I wish I could change. I really, really, really do. Profoundly. I can't. I just can't. I apologize to all of you. I think maybe you, Sam, the most.

SAM. Why me? Why most of all me?

JOHN. You seem the least defended of all of us.

SAM. I've got Sally.

SALLY. You certainly do.

CHLOE. Look at that moon! I could look at a full moon forever. I mean, next to that, all this is pretty small potatoes.

JOHN. Look next door. Everybody's dancing.

CHLOE. Thank God they still can.

SAM. You want to, honey…?

SALLY. No, thanks, I'll just listen. You go ahead. Dance with Chloe.

SAM. Come on, sis, let's borrow this music. We used to cut a mean rug. May I, John?

JOHN. She's all yours.

SAM. She always has been.

> Sam and Chloe begin to dance. They're very, very good. John comes over and sits by Sally.

JOHN. May I?

SALLY. It's a free country. That's what we're celebrating today.

JOHN. They're nice together. I like watching them.

SALLY. The doctors think I'm pregnant again.

JOHN. That's wonderful. It's what you want. What does Sam say?

SALLY. I haven't told him yet. I've disappointed him so many times.

JOHN. It's his?

SALLY. Of course.

JOHN. I'm sorry. I shouldn't have asked that. He'll be very happy.

SALLY. I hope so.

JOHN. Sure he will.

SAM. I'm going to dip you now.

CHLOE. I've had three children. Don't you dare!

He dips her.

SALLY. He knows.

JOHN. So does Chloe.

CHLOE. John, when we get home I want to get one of those bug lamps. I don't care what Betty Thompson and her ecological goon squads say, I am sick of being eaten to death by mosquitoes.

SAM. Sis, you wouldn't!

CHLOE. What has a mosquito ever done for me? Zap 'em! "Shut up and dance." That's from *Gypsy*. God, I wanna do that show one day!

SALLY. I used to hate that sound.

JOHN. The zapping? Me, too.

SALLY. Now I find it very comforting.

JOHN. Me, too.

SALLY. Zap. It's all over. Zap. Peace. Zap. No more pain.

JOHN. The end. *La commedia è finita.*

SALLY. I can hear our neighbors' even when I'm in bed. They leave it on all night. No mosquitoes on their property! We're swarming with 'em, of course. I think they can see the property line. Sam's grinding his teeth, the neighbors' bug lamp is zapping the mosquitoes, God's in His heaven, or at least our neck of New Jersey, and all's right with the world. I helped David to die. Sam doesn't know that. I don't want him to ever.

JOHN. You've got it.

SALLY. How sick are you?

JOHN. Very.

SALLY. I'm sorry.

JOHN. Zap.

SALLY. Zap.

> *They sit quietly and look out to the sea. Sam and Chloe are dancing a slow foxtrot now.*

SAM. Sis, I don't want to have children. Don't say anything. I know that's hard for you but just listen: I'm scared they won't love me. I'm scared I won't know how to raise them. Two little eyes looking up at me! Needing me, trusting me. I don't want that responsibility. I don't believe in enough to be a father. I don't have anything to give or teach. I'm empty. I'm just coasting. You don't love "empty." Please, I don't want you to say anything. This isn't about answers.

CHLOE. They would love you. You would be a wonderful father.

SAM. I wish I could believe that. How am I going to tell Sally?

CHLOE. I hope you never will.

> *They stop dancing.*

JOHN. Zap.

SALLY. Zap.

SAM. Maybe you're right, honey. Maybe we should get one of these lamps.

SALLY. Zap.

JOHN. Zap.

SAM. Zap.

> *Chloe sees a shooting star on the horizon.*

CHLOE. Look! A shooting star!

SAM. Where?

CHLOE. There!

SAM. Oh!

SALLY. Oh!

JOHN. Oh!

> *They freeze. The opening music, the trio from Mozart's* Così fan tutte *is heard again, only this time it comes from all over the theatre. It begins slowly but will get louder and louder.*

As it gets louder, both the stage lights and the house lights will come up to full intensity. The actors still have not moved. Their eyes are fixed on that distant star, their fingers pointing to it. The stage and the theatre are blazing. Audience and actors are in the same bright light. The music reaches a climax. All the lights snap off.

End of Play

PROPERTY LIST

(Use this space to create props lists for your production)

SOUND EFFECTS
(Use this space to create sound effects lists for your production)

Note on Songs/Recordings, Images, or Other Production Design Elements

Be advised that Dramatists Play Service, Inc., neither holds the rights to nor grants permission to use any songs, recordings, or other third-party design elements mentioned in the play, *including but not limited to songs from musicals*. It is the responsibility of the producing theater/organization to obtain permission of the copyright owner(s) for any such use.

For the musical Chloe is performing in, whose songs we hear on the cassette player, the title mentioned on page 59 may be changed to reflect the musical numbers used in production.

For any songs/recordings, images, or other design elements mentioned in the play, works in the public domain may be substituted. It is the producing theater/organization's responsibility to ensure the substituted work is indeed in the public domain. Dramatists Play Service, Inc., cannot advise as to whether or not a song/arrangement/recording, image, or other design element is in the public domain.

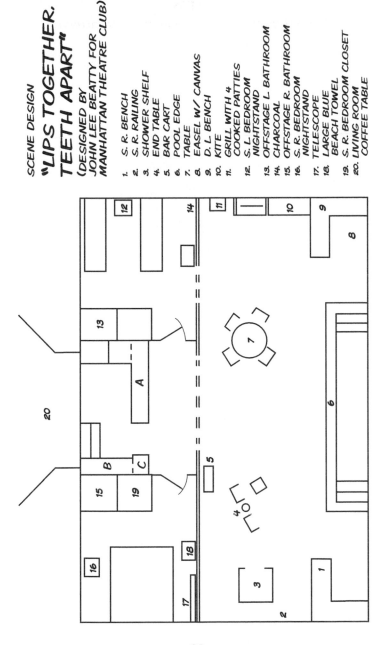

SCENE DESIGN

"LIPS TOGETHER, TEETH APART"

(DESIGNED BY
JOHN LEE BEATTY FOR
MANHATTAN THEATRE CLUB)

1. S. R. BENCH
2. S. R. RAILING
3. SHOWER SHELF
4. END TABLE
5. BAR CART
6. POOL EDGE
7. TABLE
8. EASEL W/ CANVAS
9. D.L BENCH
10. KITE
11. GRILL WITH 4
    COOKED PATTIES
12. S. L BEDROOM
    NIGHTSTAND
13. OFFSTAGE L BATHROOM
14. CHARCOAL
15. OFFSTAGE R. BATHROOM
16. S. R. BEDROOM
    NIGHTSTAND
17. TELESCOPE
18. LARGE BLUE
    BEACH TOWEL
19. S. R. BEDROOM CLOSET
20. LIVING ROOM
    COFFEE TABLE

99

NOTES
(Use this space to make notes for your production)